THE ACCEPTABLE FACE OF FEMINISM

The Women's Institute as a Social Movement

What is a Women's Institute?
  Well deary deary me
Do you think a crowd of Women
  Invited out for tea?
Is it just a village gossip
  To talk the latest news,
To whisper Village scandal?
  And every one abuse?
Why no its famous motto
  Is known far and wide
It is For Home and Country
  So rally to its side
They give some splendid lectures,
  And demonstrations too,
You'd be surprised the things they say
  And show you how to do.
They teach you how to mend your shoes,
  Make gloves and mend a hat
Cook cabbages, make sweets, cook fish
  Repair a worn out mat.
They teach you household jobbing
  First aid in case of need
The many things they teach you
  Is very great indeed
We're not all out for learning.
  There's songs and music too.
And tea the joy of every heart
  Brooke Bond's most famous brew.
We have a competition
  To try our skill and power,
When that is done I'm sure you'll own
  We've had a splendid hour.

Written by a Herefordshire member and
published in *Home and Country* in 1926

THE ACCEPTABLE FACE OF FEMINISM

The Women's Institute as a Social Movement

MAGGIE ANDREWS

Lawrence & Wishart
LONDON

Lawrence & Wishart Limited
99a Wallis Road
London E9 5LN

First published 1997
Copyright © Lawrence & Wishart, 1997

British Library Cataloguing in Publication Data.
A catalogue record for this book is available from the British Library.

ISBN 0-85315-833-9

Photoset in North Wales by
Derek Doyle & Associates, Mold Clwyd.
Printed and bound in Great Britain by
Redwood Books, Trowbridge, Wiltshire.

CONTENTS

ABBREVIATIONS

ACWW	Associated Countrywomen of the World
AGM	Annual General Meeting
AOS	Agricultural Organisation Society
BSI	British Safety Institution
NFWI	National Federation of Women's Institutes
NHS	National Health Service
NSEC	National Society for Equal Citzenship
NUWSS	National Society of Women's Suffrage Societies
TWG	Townswomen's Guilds
VCA	Village Clubs Association
VCO	Voluntary County Organiser
WAAF	Women's Auxillary Airforce
WEA	Workers Education Association
WI	Women's Institute
WILPF	Women's International League of Peace and Freedom
WSPU	Women's Social and Political Union
WVS	Women's Voluntary Service

PREFACE

Five years ago, one of my students told me she thought every woman was a bit of a feminist. This book is about a group of such women, although they are rarely associated with feminism – women who are both rural and primarily home and family oriented. In recent years there has been a growth in feminist history but the rural women of the twentieth century have received little attention. It is my aim to help rectify this omission by examining The National Federation of Women's Institutes.

I have been fortunate to gain access to the National, East Sussex and West Sussex Federations of Women's Institutes archives, as well as those at Denman College. Together with local Institutes and WI members who have shared their histories with me, I have had a wealth of sources to draw upon, for which I am very grateful. Thank you to all those who helped make these sources available and also to thank the British Library, Inter-Library Loan, the Fawcett Library and Sussex University Library.

The suggestion that I study the Women's Institute Movement came from Alun Howkins. I'd like to thank him for his support and sharing with me a belief that the Women's Institute Movement really is significant. Thanks also to friends at Sussex University and Chichester Institute, particularly Andy Medhurst whose patient proofreading and encouragement have made this book possible.

My interest in the Women's Institute Movement grew out of my own concerns as both a rural housewife and feminist. The writing of this book, therefore, owes an obvious debt to my four children. Lynton, Oliver, Dominic and Annie are hereby thanked for their tolerance and their, most of the time, goodnatured acceptance of the many hours I have had to work. Those who have looked after my children are too numerous to mention but without the practical and emotional support of Gill, Alison, Chris and my father this book would never have even neared completion. Lastly, I want to thank Neil – without whose support this book would never have been written and to whom it is dedicated.

INTRODUCTION

This book examines the Women's Institute (WI) Movement from its formation in 1915, just before the extension of the franchise to women over thirty, through the first forty-five years of its life to the eve of the emergence of the second wave of overt feminism. Although the National Federation of Women's Institutes (NFWI) is the largest women's organisation in Britain it has received no systematic academic study. Given the proliferation of women's history in the last twenty years, this is both a sad and a significant omission. Its very size and the millions of women who have been members are adequate justification for a study of the Movement.

The title *The Acceptable Face of Feminism* indicates that the emphasis of my argument is to place the NFWI as part of a much broader women's movement. Indeed my claim is that it was a significant feminist organisation. This study therefore attempts not only to challenge common sense perceptions of the NFWI but also perceptions of feminism. At first glance nothing could be further apart than the notion of the Women's Institute Movement as all about 'Jam and Jerusalem', and the popular tabloids' perception of feminists as 'hysterical shrews' or 'Dungaree Dykes'. However it is my contention that the NFWI is intrinsically linked with feminism. A biographical example may serve to illustrate the point. Edith Rigby was born in 1873, the daughter of a Preston doctor. Her suffragette activities included planting a bomb in the Liverpool Corn Exchange, pouring acid on the green of a local golf course, and setting fire to the stands of Blackburn Rovers Football Club. These resulted in her being a guest at His Majesty's pleasure some seven times. During her imprisonment she went on hunger strike and consequently suffered forced feeding. After setting fire to Lord Leverhulme's house at Rivington Pike in 1913 she declared from the dock –

> I want to ask Sir William Lever whether he thinks his property on Rivington Pike is more valuable as one of his superfluous houses occasionally opened to people or as a beacon lighted to King and Country to see here are some intolerable grievances for women.[1]

Edith was a committed socialist, entertaining Keir Hardie amongst others. A contemporary claimed of her –

> Edith was very critical of her neighbours in Winkley Square where she lived with her doctor husband, Charles. They confined their servants to the attics or basements during non working hours. Her own maids had the run of the house, eating in the dining room having the evenings free and did not wear uniforms which Edith considered badges of servitude.[2]

When World War One started Edith bought a cottage with two acres just outside Preston and began doing her bit to increase the nation's food supply. By the 1920s she was a founder member and President of Hutton and Howith WI in Lancashire. Her progression from suffrage work to the Women's Institute Movement was by no means unique. High-profile suffragettes, Virginia Woolf,[3] Elizabeth Robins, author of *The Convert* and *Votes for Women*,[4] as well as Mrs Auerbach, treasurer of the National Union of Women's Suffrage Societies (NUWSS), were all involved in the NFWI in the 1920s and 1930s. The NFWI was the largest women's movement in the post-suffrage era, to women of the period it was a natural outlet for their feminist activities. As Ray Strachey points out in *The Cause* –

> It is not too much to say that the lives of country women were transformed by the coming of this organisation, which brought instruction and variety just at the moment when enfranchisement and short skirts were bringing physical and mental development; and it is not surprising that women of all ages and classes who had worked in the suffrage movement turned their energies to this field.[5]

In order to try and understand why this organisation, now associated more with tweeds and twin sets than feminism, was seen as a natural continuation of suffrage work, I have found it necessary to ask questions about the nature of feminism and its relationship to debates about class, Englishness, leisure, consumerism and popular culture. This book is intended to be a contribution to debates about feminism and is therefore predicated upon debates about what constitutes feminist activity and whether recent definitions of feminism are applicable to the past. My first chapter – Whose Feminism? – questions the role of feminist history and how feminism can be defined, indeed, this is a theme to which I shall return frequently within the book unapologetically.

The Women's Institute Movement was an exclusively rural organisation and the particularities of this must always be borne in mind. Indeed, the very existence of a meeting of between thirty and a hundred members of a women's group within a village in the 1920s, or even now, precipitates a change in rural life, and the re-location of village space is important in removing women's perceived isolation within their own homes. Within the village a local WI provided for the development of hitherto unknown female networks, the focus of which was often the village hall – rather than the pub as previously. Therefore one obvious methodology for exploring the significance of the movement would have been to draw on Community Studies. This I have not chosen to do. The sociology of communities I believe is racked with difficulties and limitations. The very word community carries with it positive cultural codifications; it is often perceived as supportive, close knit and companionable. As Raymond Williams points out:

> Community can be a warmly persuasive word to describe an existing set of relationships, or a warmly persuasive word to describe an alternative set of relationships. What is most important, perhaps is that unlike all other terms of social organisation (state, nation etc.) It seems never to be used unfavourably, and never to be given any positive opposing or distinguishable term.[6]

It carries also, even in much of the academic work, a nostalgic notion. The real community is often under threat or just passed out of existence and yet any definition of community is singularly elusive. Newby and Bell found over ninety definitions,[7] some of which contained common characteristics such as self-sufficiency, common life and possession of common ends, norms and means. Many such community studies are very empirically based and do not overtly lay claim to a theoretical framework. They often suffer from an assumed functionalism, that is, a notion that the community concerned is made up of interrelated and dependent parts each of which serves a useful function for the other parts. This model allows little space for conflict, contestation, power, exploitation or any material basis to relationships. In not looking for such areas researchers are unlikely to find them. In laying claim to a non-political basis Community Studies work may in fact become an argument for tradition; a maintenance of the status quo, or even for a regressive golden – ageism.

The NFWI was the largest Women's Organisation in the post-suffrage era, its most distinctive feature was that it was for women only. It campaigned for many causes which are associated with more overt feminism. Furthermore, as I intend to argue, its history is one of conflict and contestation at local and national level. To try and place its study within a Community Studies approach would I feel do the organisation a limiting injustice. Another approach to the Women's Institute Movement would have been to focus on the organisation as such: its numerical growth, its leadership battles, its stated policies and how they changed. This has been the approach of many very worthy histories of women's organisations such as that on the Townswomen's Guild.[8] Indeed, my second chapter takes this area as its focus. It looks at the formation of the actual organisational structure of the movement in the early years from 1915 to the mid-1920s. Organisationally the movement has changed little from that period until the present day. An organisational emphasis may be an approach which is easier to take when the credentials of the movement do not need justification, for example if the study is on suffrage groups or the Women's Co-operative Guild. The NFWI falls into a different category. Within our culture women's organisations tend to be extremised and perceived as the threatening 'other' or trivialised; such as the Women's Institute Movement. To many women in the NFWI between 1915 and 1960 the organisation was a hugely important part of their lives. It was very significantly a space with women's values and norms and many women never missed a meeting except literally for the birth of a child or the death of their mother. To trivialise the Women's Institute Movement as 'Jam and Jerusalem' is therefore to trivialise them. To quote E.P. Thompson they need 'rescuing from the condescension of posterity'.[9] Why women joined the Movement and what it meant to them must be, therefore, a significant area of focus if these women are to be rescued from condescension. If their views or policies do not win immediate sympathy from a modern readership then that may be a reason to explore them in even more depth.

One way to get a sense of what it meant to be a member of the Women's Institute Movement at different points in time is to focus on the changing perception of the NFWI expressed through the constant re-writing of their history from 1925 to 1953. For this reason I have chosen to give this subject a whole chapter in order to provide an historical overview of the changes of emphasis within the movement that their histories encapsulate. Admittedly it is a top heavy version, that of the leadership's changing perception of the organisation and how they wanted the external world to perceive the movement. The histories illuminate the tension within the movement due to the twin association with feminism and perceptions of the 'nation' and Englishness expressed in their motto 'For Home and Country'. These histories indicate there were very real changes in the issues which were prioritised by the members and the leadership of the movement at different points in time, from food production and community service in the early period, to consumerism and flower arranging in the 1950s. Therefore the following five chapters concentrate on differing themes, concerns and pre-occupations of the movement, three of which are categorised according to the period in which they apply – the inter-war years, wartime and finally the post-war period. My aim is to understand what it might have meant to be an NFWI member at different points in time, the appeal of membership and its feminist potential. These three chapters are however interspersed with two case studies. The first case study is an example of NFWI agitation for social welfare legislation to improve the material well being of rural women in relation to housing and water supplies. It illuminates how involvement in such campaigns helped women to change their perceptions of themselves. It also indicates the potential role voluntary organisations may have in challenging and building consensus around the role and responsibility of Government in a developing welfare state. The second case study looks at Denman College, the NFWI residential college established in the post-war era, how it became perhaps a politically regressive icon for the movement but how for the women who attended it was a unique space where they could explore and develop their own capacities and confidence without male scrutiny or demands. Hence, like all the other chapters, it explores the feminist potential of the college and so of the NFWI.

I believe the NFWI was undoubtedly a feminist movement, however it spanned many of the traditional divides and groups of feminists. It attempted to challenge the boundaries of the socially constructed role for women in a number of ways, politically, economically and in cultural terms. Within the organisation there was always tension between different groups. In class and political terms there were women of all political allegiances. There were regional differences too. This created, at least until the 1950s, a creative tension. By the the external circumstances had changed, for example, the failure of the 1945 Labour Government to do very much for women, the changing class make-up of many rural villages within reach of London and the growth of consumer spending all played a part in changing the nature of the Women's Institute Movement. The year 1960 has therefore been used as the cut off point, as in many respects the organisation in the 1960s and 1970s (in the rapid growth of consumerism, mass communication and the emergence more radical and overt forms of pressure group politics) became very different in nature. After 1960 it certainly lost its primacy in the lives of rural women and began to take on more of the middle-aged and middle-class focus that it is known for today. It may therefore be helpful to briefly outline the nature of the Women's Institute Movement itself.

The movement originated in 1915 under the auspices of the Agricultural Organisation Society and reached complete independence by 1918. By 1925 it had a quarter of a million members; a figure it has never since dropped below. It would be entirely wrong to perceive its membership during this period as homogeneous. Women of all social classes from their teens to their nineties joined although predictably the leadership was middle class, though by no means exclusively. Women's Institutes then as now were village-based and run by a committee with their activities centred on a monthly meeting. This meeting was held either in an afternoon or evening and lasted two or three hours. It began with 'the business', which would refer to the organisation of the institute, county and national WI issues and any campaigns they were involved in. Then followed one, possibly two, talks or demonstrations. The topics were wide ranging. For example, North Leigh in Oxfordshire in the early 1920s covered the use of paper patterns, co-operative buying, local history, where does food come from, hay box cookery and a lecture on the Empire, amongst other matters. In 1926 their programme included local government and women voters, sightseeing in Italy, Jerusalem in the present time and the WI Movement, whereas Llanfair in 1919 had a talk on Bolshevism in its simplest form.[10] After tea, known as 'the cement' of the movement, there was a social half-hour involving dancing, singing or games. Almost every meeting had some sort of competition, for example, the best buttonhole, the best inexpensive Christmas gift. Most institutes also had a sales table where members could sell produce. Institutes also held classes. In 1920 North Leigh held classes in basket making, resoling and reheeling boots, country dancing and upholstery. Many had drama groups and choirs. In the interests of raising funds and for other reasons the local WI's also arranged a variety of other events: flower shows, whist drives, yearly outings for members, to name but a few. To some it may not sound a very significant area of feminist struggle. In the next chapter I shall try to explain why I think it is.

NOTES

1. Piers Dugden, *Village Voices*, Collins, London 1989, p19.
2. *ibid*
3. Archive File NFWI archives (see Bibliography note for the organisation of various WI archives.)
4. Elizabeth Robins, *Votes for Women* also published as *The Convert*, 1907, reprinted Virago, London 1980.
5. Ray Strachey, *The Cause*, 1928, reprinted Virago, London 1969.
6. Raymond Williams, *Keywords*, Fontana, London 1983, p66.
7. H. Newby and C.R. Bell, *Community Studies*, Allen and Unwin, London 1971.
8. M. Stott, *Organisation Women*, Macmillan, London 1978.
9. E.P. Thompson, *The Making of the English Working Class*, Penguin, Harmondsworth 1978.
10. History File NFWI archive.

1

WHOSE FEMINISM?

When I first started research into the Women's Institute Movement I
felt as a feminist that an attempt to uncover an alternative version of
the past for women was significant. On the basis of numbers alone, the
NFWI deserved to be recovered, to be no longer 'hidden from
history'.[1] My impetus for research was part of a broadening perception
of history, in the last twenty-five years a series of challenges have
emerged to the definition of the history often from the overtly
politically motivated, for example: labour history, gay history, oral
history, black history, cultural history, feminist and women's history.
These new histories were not limited to the history departments of
academic institutions, indeed many have flourished in adult education
such as the WEA and through the enthusiasm of people engaged in
disciplines such as sociology, English literature and cultural studies. I
belong to a tradition of women often engaged to some degree in
teaching in adult education, who enjoyed feminist history and felt that
creating an alternative 'truth', a more 'real' history that included
women, was part of a wider feminism. But in recent years feminism has
become to some *passé*, outmoded or irrelevant, indeed post-feminism
is now discussed. The postmodern condition, which has emerged as a
result of these challenges to notions of truth and a deconstruction of
any notion of the 'real', has, according to Raphael Samuel, 'put all
history's taken for granted procedures into question'[2] – whereas for
Jane Flax[3] it signifies the end of history. It is necessary in this first
chapter to argue that feminist history has still got a role to play in
this postmodern world and explore the perception of feminism and
feminist history upon which this book is based. (Those with more
interest in the Women's Institute Movement than feminism may
however choose to skip this chapter.)

The postmodern condition according to Judith Squires involves:

> the rejection of all essentials and transcendental conceptions of human

nature; the rejection of the pursuit of the real and the true. In place of these illusory ideals we find the assertion that man is social, historical, or linguistic artefact; the celebration of fragmentation, particularity and difference; the acceptance of the contingent and the apparent.[4]

Postmodernism announces the end of all grand narratives from modernism to Marxism, religion to racism. Truth is an impossibility or a construct. Benhabib claims postmodernism is 'infinitely sceptical and subversive in its attitude to normative claims and institutional justice and political struggles'.[5] Individuals in a postmodern world may playfully construct meaning and identity as they wish from the fragmented shopping mall world around them. As a feminist I find some appealing elements in postmodernist theory, a scepticism about an essentialist concept of human nature, or a male-defined truth or reality, for example. Arguably the identity of feminism and of women as marginalised groups has always been fragmented and the concept of rationality has always been a little problematic for women – irrationality has been a common insult that men to throw at women. Whereas I accept that all experience is represented in a selective way, that as an outsider to any experience the historian can only encounter the images and narratives of that experience and not the reality, that does not seem to me to necessitate the abandonment of the concepts of either reality or history. Arguably in a British context the postmodern playful shopping mall world from which individuals construct meaning and identity is a luxury of only a few privileged, white, bourgeois, heterosexual, southern men in work. I want to argue against ignoring the 'reality' of power and oppression, against the 'deconstruction of all principled positions'.[6] There are indeed numerous selective narratives of women's low pay, of women's unpaid and exploitive domestic labour and their sufferings of both physical and emotional domestic violence. What is needed however is to see less scepticism about feminism's political struggles to challenge such abuses of power – not more.

In this fragmented world with no sense of the 'real' or of the 'truth' surely the place of feminism and feminist history is to prevent the struggles of women (like those in the WI) to improve their lives from being dismissed. I accept that history is not about the uncovering of truth or reality but is fundamentally political; its practice is part of the covert and overt political struggles between classes, races and genders. Historians do not go and burrow away in archives to uncover the past unquestioningly. They go to those archives with certain questions framed in their minds and those questions – in an Althusserian notion of the problematic[7] – suggest exploration of certain areas of a debate whilst silencing other voices. That is fine so long as no one pretends it to be otherwise and there is a constant interrogation of what is being silenced and why. History is not just framed by the now; it is an interactive process – it frames the now. It can be a powerful weapon in the struggle over notions of common sense, over the normal, over the natural and over tradition. It forms a basis in the marshalling of consent and the creation of consensus and is a crucial tool in the maintenance of any hegemonic power bloc. A sense of history both legitimates and validates cultural practices, nationality, institutions of power, class, race and gender divisions. Hence, for women the arguments used to justify a post World War Two version of motherhood as 'traditional', or as 'natural', rely upon a historical construction or possibly even a fabrication of motherhood in the past. The political right continues to engage in a struggle for the use of the past in order to justify its politics of the present. Thatcherism, for example, mobilised a version of history – with so-called Victorian values, traditional families and notions of community (which owe a great deal to the oral history movement) in order to develop a populist consent for the dismantling of the welfare state.[8] This uncritical recovering of notions of working-class communities is in real danger of romanticising poverty and making the concept of community care, for example, rather less problematic than it ought to be.

Feminist history must operate and create spaces within which it is not marginalised as 'the Other', and in which it can inform women's fight against internalisation of their oppression and can create a history which will help women challenge the boundaries of femininity. Indeed, if the notion of history's role as being a contribution to the creation of consensus is accepted, then this is vital. To do this it must be a history available not just to a small academic elite but one which will engage in the economic, political and ideological struggles as an integral part of the culture of this society. One of the ways it can do so is by the production of the feminist historical novel, like Zoë Fairbairn's *Stand We at Last*,[9] another intention may be television series like *A Skirt Through History*, but surely this is not the only way? Feminists have to create new discourses, new ways of working, a firm commitment to accessibility, a movement away from polemical history and towards a plurality of voices and a celebration of their simultaneous fragmentation and cohesion which is what the feminist movement should be about today and, I want to argue, has always been about.

For feminists the use of history is particularly poignant. Within the prevailing culture of any historical period there are dominant notions of the feminine or what it is to be a woman. These are not straightforward and merely prescriptive but rather they allow an element of choice within boundaries or limits. Hence, for example, in the 1990s women are perceived to have a choice between being a working mother or to be a stay-at-home mother, but society still considers that the primary responsibility for children is assumed to be that of the woman. The limits or boundaries of acceptable femininity are constantly the site of struggle and of renegotiation. They vary according to class, race, regionality, sexuality, age, marital status and historic specificity. They may overlap in some areas with the boundaries of masculinity. However, what is within the boundaries of the feminine is always considered to have less status and power and is always subordinate and marginal – women always remain as 'Other'. I perceive feminist history as part of the process of challenging the boundaries of the socially constructed role of women in our society – a process which through struggle will create for women a different notion of the normal and the natural and a different tradition of being female. The political role of history means that this tradition must be one which can be empowering for women today. There will always be struggle between those upholding different versions of the past. Postmodernism may be sceptical of the 'truth' of any versions of the past, but feminists are all too aware of the power relationships which utilise different narratives to construct suitable pasts for dominant groups (or factions of dominant groups) rather than for subordinate groups, whether subordination is based on gender, race or class. Over time radical versions of the past are incorporated into the mainstream, under sufferance, within boundaries which attempt to neutralise them. It is disturbing how easily alternative meanings and readings may be placed on historical sources both primary and secondary in the battle for political credibility. Historical narratives of oppression and struggle can become incorporated into a Whig version of history – of things getting slowly better, barring a few hiccups, until now. For example, women have obtained the vote, education and birth control and with just a few minor adjustments they will have equality, won't they!

4

Furthermore, narratives of oppression and poverty in the past can serve to invalidate oppression in the present which is found by comparison lacking in the appropriate iconography. To quote Roger Bromley in *Lost Narratives*: 'The rediscovery of extensive poverty in our time has been ideologically blocked by a corresponding re-discovery of that real poverty at a time when it was nobody's fault when they were poor'.[10] There is a very real danger of exactly the same happening with a history of women's oppression; women become unable to be seen as oppressed now because they are not burdened by multiple pregnancies, denied the vote and pressed into domestic service at the age of ten. Many women know from bitter experience that male domination is not a thing of the past. Furthermore there were no pure victims in the past; as now, there was always struggle. It is as a history of struggle, either covert or overt, with space for human agency (not just victims) that feminist women's history must be perceived.

Indeed in studying the Women's Institute Movement I have been led to try and explore new areas and approaches within a feminist framework and thus try to recreate a suitable and empowering past for women today. These concerns have obviously been framed by my own feminist commitment and lived experience in the 1980s and 1990s. I have adopted two main approaches, firstly to rework perceptions of what constitutes feminism – its relationship to domesticity, networks and all-women groups. Secondly I have used the theoretical frameworks developed within popular culture to see Women's Institutes as a site for the contestation of definitions of femininity. I want to first address ways of rethinking what may be perceived as feminism. As Jenny Taylor has pointed out, 'Feminism, along with the rest of the left in Britain, currently faces a crisis that is at once theoretical and strategic, about how to define itself – a crisis that hinges most obviously on the terms identity and difference'.[11] The identity and difference defining feminism are constantly being re-negotiated, by feminists, by their supporters and opponents and by the media, of course. My own perspective of what constitutes a feminist organisation and from which I feel able to reclaim the Women's Institute Movement as feminist, is based on where I perceive the women's movement to be today, on my own personal perception of involvement in it, and what appears to make sense is to regard as feminist any activities by groups of women which challenge the boundaries of feminine behaviour whether in economic, political, or cultural terms. Such movements are not usually separate, but linked loosely, maybe by networks of women or, within umbrella organisations. I regard struggle as something which may be overt or covert, without a notion that one is somehow more real than the other. Indeed for women, covert struggle or struggle over meaning of the dominant culture may be the only avenue open to them.

Feminism is certainly fragmented on race and class lines but also around disability, sexual identity, motherhood, and within feminism between academic feminists and those who do not perceive themselves to be so. But maybe it is also necessary to create a version of feminism which incorporates women who would not describe themselves as feminists, but who struggle in a variety of areas for improvements in the lives of women, or against male domination; organisations as varied as Association for the Improvement in Maternity Services, The National Childbirth Trust, The 300 Group, Women's International League for Peace and Freedom, Women Against Pit Closures, mothers and toddlers groups, Women Against Violence Against Women, those involved in fighting the recurrent attempts to change the abortion laws and many more. That they do not all hold the same views is fine, that there is opposition between them may be seen as positive, responsible for a creative tension. Furthermore there may be significant networks between feminist organisations and groups of women. There were networks between suffrage organisations as Liz Stanley's book on Emily Wilding Davison has disclosed.[12] Shifts in personnel between groups undermines the notion of any very clear-cut polemical divisions between the suffrage groups. Maybe I am a cynic but I know if I had been alive at the time of the suffrage campaigns my allegiance would have had more to do with my already existing networks of women, what fitted in with childcare arrangements, or was close to available transport than ideological purity. A notion of women organising, surviving, and supporting each other through networks is vital to feminist historical analysis. As Mary Ryan argues, 'Within segregated female spheres and women's networks they [feminist historians] have discerned evidence of the ability of women to maximise their freedom and exert considerable social influence'.[13] In looking at an organisation like the NFWI such considerations must be borne in mind. Class was a significant division between the women but this must not undermine the role played by middle-class women in improving the conditions of working-class women's lives. Women's oppression is differentiated on historical, class, regional, and racial grounds, however; if the slogan 'the personal is political' is to have any meaning women must speak from where they are positioned. In looking at women's history it is necessary to be sympathetic to this, which doesn't mean that what women say is necessarily insular. On the contrary, it is all inter-related, all part of the same struggle. To try and divide and categorise feminists may result in a massive loss of complexity, furthermore there is also a danger in presenting a notion of the women's movement in the past as more uniform (if rather small and spasmodic). This can be unhelpful and produce golden-ageism and a nostalgia for periods of 'true' feminist movements, for example, prior to the suffrage bill or in the 1960s. Then, apparently, there were cohesive women's movements, at least according to some very narrow definitions of what political movements are, a problem Martin Pugh's limited male history of twentieth-century feminism suffers from.[14] By such standards of apparent cohesion feminism today may be perceived as a failure or non-existent. Feminism, like any other movement of a subordinate group, has always been fragmented, at one linked and divided, held together by networks and very loose communalities. This may be a weakness, but it can also be a strength. Indeed, the WI's ability to be a popular movement relied upon it being able to serve the needs of different groups and to articulate the demands of a variety of groups in class and regional terms.

In trying to assess feminism in the post-1915 era and the WI's place within it, I have found the first stage, for me, has been to be wary of some of the categories and definitions, even orthodoxies, which suround notions of the feminist movement in this country between 1918 and 1960. The most significant of these is that there was not one. In a period of time when post-feminism is spoken about, this is an interesting notion. The original orthodoxy was that after 1918 the women's movement fell apart not to be seen again until the 1960s. Individual or outstanding women have been focused upon but rarely was there a sense of women's movement.[15] This was replaced by a new orthodoxy following in the wake of feminist books like Dale Spender's, *There's Always Been a Woman's Movement This Century*.[16] Instead, women diffused into a variety of other organisations, particularly those of the left. Apparently women who campaigned for women's issues in the post-suffrage era could be divided into two groups. First the older style liberal or equal rights feminists who wanted equal pay, educational opportunities for women, entry into the professions and the removal of any legislation which distinguished between men and women, even protective work related legislation.

Alternatively, there were the new social or maternal feminists who argued for the improvement of facilities for women as mothers, particularly in social terms; for example, maternity services, child benefit and birth control. Women such as Eleanor Rathbone who campaigned for allowances for children and mothers would be seen in this category. This social feminism was seen by Beddoe as having a dominant influence upon feminism until the 1960s.[17] My examination of the NFWI, has led me to reject these divisions between women in the period between World War One and 1960. The more I have looked at the Women's Institute Movement the more I came to realise that the networks and links between women's groups are numerous. For example, Virginia Woolf, whose books Three Guineas[18] and *A Room of One's Own*[19] must rate her as an important feminist theorist of the period, has been linked with the Women's Co-operative Guild. In the late 1930s and 1940s she was involved with her local East Sussex WI and became its treasurer. I believe it is vital that the NFWI be seen as a continuum of the more overtly politicised women's movements both before and in parallel with it. Equal rights issues such as the campaigns for women police and equal pay, and demands for improved maternity services (a classic social/maternal feminist campaign) were all on the NFWI agenda. In terms of personal issues and cultural codification there were networks and links going on between a wide variety of women's movements in the 1920s, 1930s and 1940s. Thus, women such as Eleanor Rathbone, Virginia Woolf and Elizabeth Robins[20] tended to move from one organisation to another, to prioritise one issue or group of issues, as women do now according to their political, economic and cultural specificity at a particular point in time.

The organisation did not challenge women's primarily domestic role although it certainly challenged its construction. I feel there is a real problem in the assumption that, unless an organisation rejects domesticity it can not be feminist. For the majority of rural working-class women the material reality of their lives was, and often still is, such that the world of work offers only 'women's work' which was (and often still is) badly paid, low status, part-time and with few promotion prospects. Deirdre Beddoe summarises the inter-war period thus – 'a women's place was in the home and if she went out to work it was low paid'. In the rural areas, where the Women's Institute Movement operated, the problems of limited job opportunities were exaggerated by lack of transport. The opportunities for rural women to work that had existed in the nineteenth century, explored in detail by

Pamela Horn,[21] had seriously contracted by the twentieth century. Work may therefore have had little to offer rural women in terms of liberation. What it may have offered, instead, was the double oppression of workplace and home. Domesticity and its evaluation are therefore something which must be perceived as relative. Furthermore, given that many of the women to whom the NFWI was addressing itself, had passed the point of having any choice about whether to be unpaid domestic workers or not, no movement which invalidated housewives' position would have gained much credence. Maybe this is something from which present day feminism would do well to learn. It may be that the modern women's movement's greatest success, in terms of numbers, lies where they do not challenge domesticity directly, but instead try to raise political consciousness around issues of immediate concern to women like abortion, for example.

The NFWI's perception of womanhood may have been primarily domestic but it was not a passive domesticity. It was a long way from the idealised *Angel in The House* popularised by Coventry Patmore in the nineteenth century.[22] A Lancing member writing in *Home and Country* (the NFWI magazine) claimed – 'I hold no brief for the old fashioned, devoted wife, who scuttled about like a fussy hen, looking for little jobs and manufacturing them if they did not exist'.[23] Indeed the Women's Institute Movement had a significant role to play in re-negotiating domesticity, into something which was certainly far more politically aware than previous versions. Furthermore the organisation rejected the male capitalist value system's perception of their labour as of low status and value. To the NFWI women were domestic workers and their work was equivalent to that of men. The Movement did not merely validate women's work, they attempted to raise it to the level of skilled work. Skill is to a large degree a socially constructed concept and one that is primarily associated with men. Notions of skill are also linked to job satisfaction and ideas of fulfilment – something for which domestic labour has, justifiably, an ambiguous reputation. As I shall argue later, notions of skill permeate numerous of the Movement's activities and lie behind the monthly competitions and local, county and national exhibitions. Through their WIs women could experience an alternative female value system which challenged the internalisation of dominant perceptions of skill, status and productivity.

The emphasis on domesticity within the Movement in some respects served to help it to be perceived as an acceptable leisure pursuit. The

Women's Institute Movement's perception of themselves as skilled workers helped the members to feel they had a right to leisure important in the covert agenda of the WI The leisure itself was often, on the surface, of a very traditional nature – singing, acting, folk dancing – but for women to demand this right to leisure in all female groups, and possibly the struggle to assert that right, was significant in a feminist sense. Furthermore as a group of women who saw themselves as skilled domestic workers, WI members were concerned with improving the conditions of their labour and becoming more efficient workers. Autonomy and control over their lives were perceived as important, as were co-operative activities which would improve the material conditions of life for WI members and their families. This led them to become involved in a wide variety of social welfare campaigns, one of which, for improved rural housing and water supplies, will be looked at as a case study in chapter five. I want, however, to challenge any simple explanation of the NFWI as a purely reformist organisation. Joyce Gelb argues:

> Reformist feminists seek equality through freedom – they do not seek to overturn the prevailing system, although they may be in conflict with those elements of it that they see as oppressive and hostile to women's self determination ...

whereas in talking about radical feminists she says:

> In this perspective, the only way to alter women's oppression is to transform the ideology and institutions of existing society.[24]

Such a division is not applicable to the NFWI or probably to any other organisation. They certainly challenged dominant ideologies and reformist campaigns in themselves could lead to a questioning of the political, economic and cultural structure of society.

Maybe it should therefore come as no surprise that the NFWI was castigated by both the political left and right in the 1920s for its political bias, and even by the Church of England. In Yorkshire in the 1920s husbands refused to let their wives join what they described as 'that secret society'.[25] One of the most extreme reactions came in a letter to *Home and Country* in 1928 signed a 'Mere man' and complaining about the amount of time spent on, and involvement with, the Women's Institute Movement by wives. The subtext of the letter being, presumably, that this time should be spent in dancing attendance on men. The letter writer claimed:

I mix with men, many of whom are husbands of Institute members and
the things they say about the Institute are unprintable. One told me this
morning that damned Institute is the curse of a married man's life.[26]

This letter writer obviously felt himself severely threatened and
inconvenienced by his wife's membership of the organisation. At one
level, it might be possible to explain this by reference to the threat to
men of female friendships and any activity which excludes men. Some
American feminists such as Adrienne Rich have argued that all female
friendship needs to be seen in terms of a lesbian continuum;[27] that
'women who love women, who choose women to nurture and support
and to create a living environment in which to work creatively and
independently are lesbians'.[28] Arguably more useful to any analysis of
the WI is Janice Raymond's argument that lesbian-being requires a
deliberate choice. She describes the strong female friendships, often
precipitated by shared interests or membership of a group or
organisation as gyn/affection[29] whose basic component entails women
putting other women first. This can be both supportive and
empowering for women and by the same token disempowering for
men. Certainly the Women's Institute Movement and other
women-only organisations and leisure activities can be seen as a
significant site for the development of gyn-affection.

Maybe in order to understand the level of aggression expressed by
the 'mere man' it is necessary to go beyond men's nervousness about
female friendship and look at how the Women's Institute Movement
worked in the villages to create for women an alternative cultural
space, a form of female-run counter-culture within which they
challenged perceptions of the domestic role of rural women. Women's
oppression, within a male-dominated society, works in a number of
ways. A significant contribution to the maintenance of male
dominance is in the internalisation of women's subservient position by
women themselves. The local WI created a site for women-only leisure
where women could explore their own abilities and interests away
from male censure. Within this women were supported by other
women to combat the internalisation of subservience, a sense of
'otherness' or invisibility which they might experience in more
mainstream culture spaces. Paul Tillich has argued that:

> The self-affirmation of a being, in spite of non-being, is the expression of
> its power of being. Here we are at the roots of the concept of power.

> Power is the possibility of self affirmation in spite of internal and
> external negation. It is the possibility of overcoming non-being.[30]

Women are frequently alienated, denied a sense of self and culturally
perceived as 'Other'. A space like the WI in which they can obtain a
sense of being is a space for them to obtain power and can thus be truly
feminist. The feminist potential of organisations like the NFWI may to
some significant extent lie in the meanings and interpretations that its
membership can create within it. It gives them a level of agency, a space
to find themselves away from male censure. Meanings, the way women
perceive their lives, are a site of contestation and empowerment. One
of the central tenets developed in feminist counselling and therapy in
the 1970s and 1980s was that although it was not always possible to
change women's lives or the people in them, it was possible to change
the way women saw their lives and that gave women a greater degree of
power and control. Women's groups like the NFWI provided many
women with a chance to change the way women saw their lives in just
such a way, years before. Few women's organisations, unless
outwardly radical, have received serious feminist attention and yet as
Germaine Greer remarks in relation to convents:

> I want to see women being happier in their groups and less apologetic
> for them. I like the way women laugh without self-consciousness when
> there are no men around. If you go into a pub you won't hear women
> rolling around on the floor with laughter. You'll hear the polite
> responses to men's jokes. You won't hear too many jokes by women
> either, because they're watching someone else's performance. When
> you're within convent walls or college walls then the women's innate
> creativity has to come out. So we were uproarious and the nuns were
> uproarious too. They were all droll and mad in their particular ways.
> They didn't conform to any stereotype, they were all different.[31]

This quote underlies what I see as very significant about an
organisation like the WI and its women-only status. It offers a
potential for women to be themselves, to develop their own value
system, creativity, humour and sense of self worth: as such it can not
fail to provide space for feminism. Little historical work has been done
in looking at women's groups in this way but Jill Julius Matthews's
work on the Women's Health and Beauty League sets a welcome
precedent. She explores both the development of the organisation

between the wars and also the meanings and pleasure derived from it by the members. She argues the necessity of not producing a merely organisational history which would 'tend to lose the agency of the women involved; they become a part of a mass, manipulated by supra-individual structural forces'.[32] However she also warns against an over emphasis on the individual:

> Such an inward story, however, would tend towards Trevelyan's 'history with politics left out' a timeless saga of individual consciousness. What is needed is a combination of the two directions, not a simple juxtaposition of the two movements but some sort of integration, a balancing of the social and the personal, of politics and pleasure, of structure and subjectivity.[33]

It seems to me that recent feminist work on popular culture has been more successful in attempting to move in just such a direction and that it is in this area that some of the most exiting feminist work has been produced recently; work like Janice Radway's *Reading the Romance*[34] and collections such as *The Female Gaze* which argue that change within an economic or ideological system is a slow process based upon struggle to 'shift the ground for economic change or even to make more bearable the lives of those at the sharp end of systems of oppression ... This involves centrally a struggle over meaning'.[35] The ideas of Stuart Hall[36] that popular culture is a sight of contestation over meaning and hegemony are developed to get away from a moralising notion towards women who enjoy *Neighbours* and Mills and Boon novels and explore instead – why? It has begun to see the complexity in such questions – to regard the likes of soap operas not simply as carriers of dominant ideology but as open texts – as areas with spaces for the contestation of the boundaries and meaning of femininity. Thus those exploring contemporary popular culture have been able to reclaim the feminism in Madonna and in reading romances. Alternatively feminist historians are still haunted by the suffragettes and nineteenth-century Lancashire mill girls.[37] Significant as these areas are they do not really represent the lived experience of the majority of women in the past and that maybe is why they are failing to say a great deal to the majority of women today and may not therefore be able to promote a past which inspires women today. In my wish to lay emphasis on the meaning of being a WI member I have chosen to adopt many of the theoretical premises of recent work on popular culture.

An organisation like the NFWI may seem at a superficial level to be trying to inculcate the working class with an image of womanhood that was domestic, patriotic, maternal and dedicated to trying to live out some sort of rural idyll. However, that would be to take what could be regarded as a deeply patronising attitude by perceiving the members as cultural dupes. The members of a local WI meeting were as selective in their attendance and concentration as any individual is in watching an evening's television programmes. Many members came to their WI for the social side, the educational part of the meeting – talks and lectures received a very mixed response. The records in minute books give a wide variety of subjects discussed; they also indicate that women dozed, talked and knitted through topics that didn't interest them. Furthermore, attendance numbers show a huge level of selectivity, for example Funtington WI, in the 1920, could muster over a hundred and fifty people for a dance and only thirty for a talk on making something out of nothing.[38] This is a clear indication that the participants of the Women's Institute Movement were active and selective, not passive recipients of ideology. To see popular culture as a site of contestation it is necessary to be aware of the degree of autonomy the relatively powerless have. The women who attended the NFWI were carving out a space in their lives which meant something to them and within which they could work out alternative meanings for the structure of their lives. What it meant may bear little relation to what the Board of Agriculture or similar bodies involved in the early promotion of the WI perceived it to mean.

Following these theoretical premises much of what follows is about different meanings that NFWI activities may suggest and the struggle over these meanings. At one level these readings and interpretation of WI activities and texts are selective, they are not a definitive truth. I have not however abandoned the academic practise of history but rather I am attempting to be overt about its process. In the historical sources I used, I looked for a version of reality which would be empowering for women today. This interpretation argues that WI members were able to use the organisation for feminist ends. Thus it is my contention that the Women's Institute Movement was a significant, and certainly the largest, feminist organisation in the post-suffrage era. Its mass appeal, based in many respects on their re-appropriation of domesticity, has a lot to say to feminism today; by recapturing the feminist potential of some truly popular movements, feminism might now be able to move itself towards a wider appeal. I hope that setting an organisation like the NFWI within concepts such as networks and a plurality of voices, a different perception of feminism in the past can be obtained. The women in the movement struggled in national political terms and locally to improve the material circumstances of women's lives. Perhaps most importantly, through the formation of a female subculture within rural villages they provided a space for women to fight the internalisation of male domination and to adopt an alternative value system. It is an example that feminism today would do well to remember.

NOTES

1. S. Rowbotham, *Hidden from History*, Pluto Press, London 1973.
2. R Samuel, 'Reading the Signs', *History Workshop Journal* 33, 1992, p220.
3. J. Flax, *Psychoanalysis Feminism and Post Modernism in the Contemporary West*, Berkley University Press, Berkley 1990, p32-34.
4. J Squires (ed.), *Principled Positions*, Lawrence & Wishart, London 1993, p2.
5. S. Benhabib, *Situating the Self*, Polity Press, Cambridge 1992, p15.
6. J. Squires, (ed.), *op.cit.*
7. R.Johnson, 'Three Problematics', in J. Clarke, C. Critcher, R. Johnson, *et al* (eds.), *Working Class Culture*, Hutchinson, London 1979, p201.
8. R. Samuel, (ed.), *Patriotism – The Making and Unmaking of British National Identity*, Volume 3, Routledge, London 1988.
9 Z. Fairbairn, *Stand We at Last*, Virago, London.
10. R. Bromley, *Lost Narratives*, Routledge, London 1988, p8.
11. J. Bourne Taylor, 'Raymond Williams, Gender and Generation', in T. Lovell (ed.), *British Feminist Thought*, Blackwell, Oxford 1990, p298.
12. Liz Stanley and A. Morley, *The Life and Death of Emily Wilding Davies*, Virago, London 1988.
13. Mary Ryan, 'The Power of Women's Networks', in J. Newton *et al* (eds.), *Sex and Class in Women's History*, Routledge, London 1983, p167.
14. Martin Pugh, *Women and the Women's Movement in Britain*, Macmillan, London 1992.
15.   L. Caldecott, *Women of Our Century*, Ariel Books, London 1984. also A. Neustatter, *Hyenas in Petticoats*, Harrap, London 1989.
16. D. Spender, *There's Always been a Feminist Movement This Century*, Virago, London 1983.
17. D. Beddoe, *Back to Home and Duty*, Virago, London 1989, p6.
18. V. Woolf, *Three Guineas*, 1938, reprinted Penguin, London 1982.
19. V. Woolf, *A Room of One's Own*, 1929, reprinted Granada, London 1982.
20. J. Alberti, *Beyond Suffrage*, Macmillan, London 1989.
21. P. Horn, *Ladies of the Manor*, Sutton, Stroud 1991.
22. C. Patmore, 'Angel in the House', quoted in C. Christ, 'Victorian Masculinity and the Angel in the House', in M. Vicinus (ed.), *The Widening Sphere*, Indiana University Press, Indiana 1977.

23. *Home and Country*, October 1930, p31.
24. J. Gelb, *Feminism and Politics*, University of California Press, Berkeley 1989, p31.
25. History File in NFWI archive.
26. *Home and Country*, October 1928, p524.
27. A. Rich, 'Compulsory heterosexuality and lesbian existence', in A. Snitow, *et al* (eds.), *Desire*, Virago, London 1981.
28. B.W. Cook, 'Female Support Networks and Political Activism', in *Crysalis 3*, (USA Spring 1978).
29. J. Raymond, *A Passion for Friends*, Women's Press, London 1991.
30. P. Tillich, *Love, Power and Justice*, Oxford University press, Oxford 1954, p30.
31. G. Greer, quoted in J.Bennett and R.Forgan, *There's Something About a Convent Girl*, Virago, London 1991, p89.
32. J. Matthews, 'They had such a lot of fun: The Women's League of Health and Beauty', in *History Workshop 30*, Autumn 1990 , p37.
33. *ibid*.
34. J. Radway, *Reading the Romance*, University of North Carolina Press, Chapel Hill 1994.
35. L. Gamman and M. Marshment (eds), *The Female Gaze*, Women's Press, London 1988, p2.
36. S. Hall, 'Notes towards deconstructing the Popular', in R. Samuel (ed.), *People's History and Socialist Theory*, Routledge, London 1981.
37. See for example J. Liddington and J. Norris, *One Hand Tied Behind Us*, Virago, London 1978.
38. Funtington WI minute books held by Funtington WI.

2

THE EARLY YEARS

The Women's Institute, though nowadays seeming to perpetuate notions of 'Englishness', is not in origin a British organisation; rather it is an import from the colonies founded in Canada in 1897 at Stoney Creek. The aims of this fledgling organisation were soon summed up in a resolution claiming that 'A Nation can not rise above the level of its homes; therefore we women must work and study together to raise our homes to the highest possible level'.[1] The Canadian movement was very closely linked to government and in 1911 this was formalised in an advisory board of four women appointed to the Department of Agriculture of British Columbia to 'assist the Department in forming and guiding the Institutes' with an executive officer, Mrs Watt. After the early death of her husband in 1913 Mrs Watt came to England, specifically to promote the Women's Institute Movement (a variation of the movement already existed in America and many European countries by this time). With missionary zeal she attempted to inspire a will amongst government departments, politicians, women's organisations and even society hostesses such as Lady Louise Loder, to set up WIs in Britain. However, all attempts proved futile until after the outbreak of war when Mrs Watt wrote a pamphlet on the Women's Institutes and food production.[2] Despite lectures on the subject to the League of the Empire and at a meeting of university women in London University, it required a higher level of participation in the war effort by the general public before the notion of Women's Institutes took off in England. In February 1915, Mrs Watt met Mr Nugent Harris, a Governor of the Agricultural Organisation Society (AOS) and at last found a sympathetic ear for her ideas. Mr Harris wrote:

> For many years when secretary to the AOS I tried to get the farmer members of the co-operative agricultural societies I was organising to allow women to become members, but failed. Then I got two or three to

yield. Several women joined, but we could never get them to say a word at the general meeting.

After the meetings were over the women would come to me and criticise the decisions or some of the agenda in which they were interested. I asked them why they did not have their say at the meeting. They replied 'We dare not because our husbands and sons would make fun of us.' I would not rest until I could establish some movement that would give women-folk a chance to express themselves free from the fear of being ridiculed by men. By the merest chance, I met Mrs Watt. I felt I had come in touch with the very movement I wanted.[3]

Mr Harris's altruism may be questioned but his actions cannot. In 1915, as a member of the executive of the Agricultural Organisation Society, he was instrumental in getting Mrs Watt to read a paper at the annual meeting of the AOS Mrs Watt's speech was followed by a resolution proposing that the Canadian Women's Co-operative Institutes should be adapted for British rural life and that this should be done by the AOS with the Governors becoming responsible for the work. It was one of those resolutions which passed at the end of meeting when the hall was beginning to empty and there was according to Robertson Scott's account of events, some doubt about whether those concerned knew what they were voting for.[4]

The AOS, under whose auspices the WI was started in this country, was long out-lived by its protégé. By 1915 it had been operational for three years. It was aided by government grants and had the avowed intention of promoting co-operation in agriculture. Ideas of co-operation became integral to NFWI ideals in the years to come. Indeed, its first intention was to be called the Women's Co-operative Institute. This was abandoned in deference to the Women's Co-operative Guild;[5] though a member's poem in the 1920s was to announce 'we'll raise the standard of the British Nation through our co-operation'.[6] The achievements of the AOS were not always obvious, an ex-governor later said of it

It was a period of big conceptions and the AOS somehow failed to rise to them; some of its moderate-sized geese were swans and its stationery bills were awful.... The AOS did not by its general method of work, impress the farmers as much as was necessary. It did not gain their ear, though I doubt if anybody could have done so, except perhaps the Archangel Gabriel.[7]

It was suggested that the WI would provide the very ear that was required for these farmers and smallholders. I will return to this concern with food production and agriculture later in the chapter.

While not wanting to ascribe the growth of an organisation like the WI to mere dependence on personalities, some of them did have a very significant effect upon the very early years of the movement, and Mrs Watt was undoubtedly one, although there are indications of some friction between Mrs Watt and the movement she had started later in the 1920s. Her perception of rural women owed a great deal to the Canadian Pioneer ideology[8] and frontier women as self-reliant, self-sufficient, resourceful and distanced from the taint of commercial capitalism and consumerism. Within Britain it was also influenced by a radical tradition of self-reliance which can be traced from Cobbett's *Cottage Economy* and the labour aristocracy of the nineteenth century. Mrs Watt's pioneer woman was visible in the WI thinking four years after when a member wrote – 'We want to encourage all women to be self-contained and to be able to make and mend for their own homes'.[9] This image of womanhood although still primarily domestic is a very significant renegotiation of the Victorian ideal of the 'angel in the house'. Mrs Watt was engaged by the AOS as a temporary organiser for the proposed WIs and personally set up the first one hundred Institutes. The first three were in Wales, the first in England at Singleton in West Sussex, chosen because Mrs Watt had a friend there. Women's Institutes were frequently started on the instigation of a member of the ruling elite within a village who had contact with either Mrs Watt or some other members of the AOS. They could be: doctors, vicars, shopkeepers, publicans, small and large landowners or those who ran their own small business and did not have to labour manually. The Institute Movement was not always well received, the democratic principle, (of one member one vote) horrified one lady of the manor who on discovering that she would not automatically be elected president declared 'she had no intention of allowing such a radical movement in their village'.[10]

Mrs Watt, accompanied by Mr Nugent Harris or other members of the AOS, started Institutes throughout England and Wales. Meetings were held in villages to explain the idea of a WI. The aim by the end of the meeting was to elect a committee which contained all the usual officers and would be responsible for the day to day running of the institute. It organised the programme, outings, speakers, competitions, social and fundraising events and so on. Each Institute was an independent entity with its own autonomy, not a branch of a central organisation. This enabled them to adapt and suit their activities to the needs of their own rural area, holding meetings once a month in village halls, club rooms or side rooms of pubs, either in the afternoon or the evening. Some Institutes favoured the afternoon on the basis that women could then be home in time to cook the mens' evening meal, while others favoured the evening meeting as it forced men to look after their children at least once a month. The WIs were attended by women of all social classes and concerned themselves with industry, work and all matters centred around the home, the garden, allotment or farm. The first published aims and objectives of the movement were:

1) stimulating interest in the agricultural industry
2) developing co-operative industries
3) encouraging home and local industries
4) studying home economics
5) providing a centre for educational and social intercourse and for all local activities.[11]

Individuals joined a local institute and through that the national organisation. Once an Institute was established, prospective members required a proposer and a seconder and their application was then voted on either by the local committee or the whole institute. The membership fee was two shillings annually, no more or less. It was considered a significantly democratic move that wealthier women could not pay more than this and consequently acquire an unreasonable level of influence within the Institute. (A similar practice had been adopted by some friendly societies in the nineteenth century.) No one was excluded from this membership fee however important their social standing, as rather worried and delicately phrased letters following the formation of Sandringham Institute make clear.[12]

Increases in the number of institutes occurred rapidly in 1916 and 1917. Consequently, the personnel required to deal with the WI grew. The AOS had by 1916 a subcommittee to deal with Women's Institutes chaired by Mrs Wilkins, whose main concern, was with the Farm and Garden Union. She was uneasy about the relationship of the WI to the AOS and her role within it; consequently an outsider was sought, and Mrs Wilkins's suggestion of Lady Denman was accepted. Lady

Denman (1884 – 1954) initially held her position by appointment, although later she was elected National Federation Chairman so often that to those involved with the WI she became a natural and obvious choice. In many respects she was indicative of a new more independent and progressive outlook for the movement which was to emerge in the 1920s. She was the wife of the ex-Governor General of Australia and the daughter of a wealthy and titled family. Her father was one of the newly created Liberal peers of 1911 and his involvement in politics had included support for women's suffrage. She herself was strongly in favour of agricultural small-holders and significantly was very involved in campaigns for family planning well into the 1940s. Her perception of rural womanhood differed from that of Mrs Watt; it was based upon the positive experience for women of the suffrage campaign. Her personal life does not seem to have been such as to instil in her a belief in motherhood or marriage as the be-all and end-all of women's existence.[13] Lady Denman was able to inspire an enormous amount of loyalty from rank and file members of the WI who were not necessarily even interested in, let alone in favour of, many of her views. As a member of the British aristocracy she was perceived by many as a 'natural leader' and indeed it was only in 1961 the NFWI had a non-titled chairwoman.

There was a growing discontent amongst members of the AOS that the WI was diverting too much of its energy away from the real aims. Following an unsuccessful attempt to increase the AOS grant from the Treasury; the Board of Agriculture set up a Women's Institute Section which, with Lady Denman as honorary assistant director, would 'sponsor the Institute organisation, conduct the propaganda, and form Institutes, yet leave them free when formed to manage their own affairs'.[14] The Women's Branch had not been in existence long and its chief concerns were women's seasonal work and the Women's Land Army.

Within England and Wales (Scotland had a separate organisation)[15] the clear intention was complete independence, a self-financing and democratically controlled organisation. The changes in the organisation were passed and the new rules of the Federation adopted by a conference of representatives of the 137 Women's Institutes, at Central Hall, Westminster on the afternoon of 16 October 1917. This conference was followed in 1918 by the first AGM which became the main policy-making meeting of the organisation. With the exception of wartime, the meetings have been held every year since. Any resolution with a two-thirds majority on a public question was put before the Minister concerned, those with less received further attention within the Movement. All Institutes had equal voting rights at the AGM and maximum attendance was encouraged. This was particularly so when a system for pooling fares was devised whereby the total travel costs were divided equally between all the Institutes thus trying to alleviate the financial if not the practical problems of sending a delegate from the more distant areas. The AGM soon gained national attention and was dubbed the Countrywomen's Parliament. In 1927 the *Western Morning News and Mercury* reported:

> Long before women had won the right to vote, they had established a virile parliament of their own, in which the voice of a mere man counted for nothing – except in an advisory capacity. This great parliament is, of course the Women's Institute Movement, which is holding its annual meeting in the Queens Hall this week.[16]

The move to the Board of Agriculture brought with it (even if it was only to be a temporary matter) an input of funds, personnel and official channels of publicity which reaped encouraging results. The number of institutes went up from 187 in 1917 to 1,405 in 1919. Significant in assisting in the ability to grow at such a rate was the decision to create Voluntary County Organisers (VCOs) who would operate at county level to help with the propaganda work and the formation and nurturing of new institutes. Funding was provided to organise a residential training school for the VCOs in Sussex and to pay expenses of three pounds a month to VCOs once trained. Within no time at all a formal structure developed around their appointment including written examinations. During the war period, a uniform and a hat were available for VCOs at Harrods.[17] The women who volunteered initially came from a wealthy background, as had many of the women involved in the suffrage campaigns. Many of them saw this work as their part of the war effort, their patriotic duty. As one said – 'When the request to do this work came, I accepted immediately. It was something for my country. No thought of pleasure or gain occurred to me'.[18] The writer of this letter went on to express the positive gains and enjoyment she found through her involvement in this women's organisation. The first batch of VCOs were carefully selected upper-class women, although only two were titled. Certainly those with servants, cars and other trappings of middle-class life of the period found it easier practically and had greater confidence to undertake such work. However, working-class women with the time and commitment, not to speak of the confidence to challenge the normal workings of class hegemony, were valued within the NFWI hierarchy. Mrs Alice Freeman, whose husband was a gardener, became a VCO in the 1920s. She sat on her County Committee and the National Organisation Committee. She cycled miles in her work as a VCO and helped train others. She recalled her first attendance at a meeting at headquarters:

> Well I sat at the meeting round the table and felt very uncomfortable. Then Lady Denman said 'Mrs Freeman, don't look so frightened. We are not going to eat you I will see you later'. When we adjourned for lunch she asked me what was the matter. I said 'You are all educated people and I have no proper education or anything I can't see what use I am going to be on this committee'. She said, You'll be as much use as any one of us. Education doesn't mean a thing. Its experience that counts. We go down the village streets and see all the nice doorways but we don't know what goes on behind them. This is what we need to know: what sort of life the village people have got because we want to do as much as we can.[19]

Such women were not common, but they were significant and valued. The VCOs quickly became an integral part of the WI Further training schools were held in 1918 and eleven were held in 1919, bringing the total number of VCOs up to 89.

The end of the war in 1918 brought the end of the relationship between the Board of Agriculture and the Women's Institutes. The movement, when faced with the news that they must now become completely independent, applied, with the board's backing, for a grant from the Development Commission. However, they met with difficulties. The Village Clubs Association was already receiving a grant from the Commission as it complied with 'the Cabinet Reconstruction Sub-Committee's declaration in favour of mixed clubs'. The WI was perceived, probably quite accurately, as a potential rival to the Village Clubs Association.[20] The WI Executive, supported by a resolution of a WI General Meeting, were firmly committed to a women only policy. In a compromise that was not to abolish the problem for many years, it was agreed that the WI could receive a grant provided that a joint standing committee was set up between the two organisations.

Finally in 1919, the County Federations which had grown up in some areas in an *ad hoc* fashion were brought within the national structure and invited to adopt a set of rules set up by the National Federation. Representatives of the counties also formed a Consultative Council to work whenever possible with the executive. The Consultative Council met twice a year and passed resolutions on both internal Women's Institute Movement issues and wider political issues which affected rural women. In time, they also came to have a significant role in the selection of resolutions sent in by Institutes for the NFWI AGM. Local institutes also informally associated together in what were known as 'groups'. These consisted of approximately six institutes who would organise events jointly. The National Federation were uncertain about these arrangements. It was decided that despite an unsuccessful AGM resolution in 1922 to give Local Institutes the right to representation on County Federation Committees, the existence of these groups was to be kept 'informal and extra – constitutional'.[21] By 1919 the overall structure of an independent NFWI, even if on a slightly shaky financial footing, was established. An indication of the confidence of the Movement and the attempt to build on a growing sense of cohesion can be seen in the establishment in 1919 of the NFWI monthly magazine *Home and Country* for which many County Federations provided their own local supplement. It became a central space for the organisation to establish its own identity and culture. Articles, letters, pages of local, county and national news all helped to give the diverse federal structure of the NFWI a sense of inter-relatedness and unity. The structure of the NFWI was to change little after this except for the attempt by the Village Clubs Association at an amalgamation in the 1920s.

The Village Clubs Association (VCA) came into being in 1918 with the express intention of organising village clubs and institutes consisting of men and women. From the point in 1918 when the WI was compelled to form a joint committee with the VCA relations between the two were strained. The VCA was very different in nature from the WI. It attempted to build upon village clubs and organisations already in existence, for example sports clubs. Some of those involved in the VCA in 1921 were enthusiastic for some sort of an amalgamation to take place between the WI and the VCA.[22] An end was put to any hopes of this in 1923 when an explicit resolution at the NFWI AGM declared that the Institutes shall be open to women only[23] and those men who had been involved in the leadership of the Movement either as honorary members or as elected members of the executive of the NFWI were from then on excluded. However, men did remain on the executive for a few more years as co-opted members of other organisations. In 1924 there were two men from the Board of Agriculture and one from the AOS. Despite this the 1923 resolution marks a significant point in the development of gender consciousness within the movement. A journalist writing on this AGM criticised its feminist attitude. H.B. Pointing wrote:

> It was unfortunate that some of the speakers seemed to take up the attitude that 'we must do this or that because we're women'. The inevitable result of the position is that you begin to criticise almost automatically the things men do 'because they're men!'. This zest for artificial distinctions does not, of course, characterise this women's movement only.[24]

There was undoubtedly amongst many members of the VCA (such as Mr Nugent Harris) a misguided impression that women would benefit, as well as men, from joint clubs within rural villages.

The women of the Women's Institute Movement, whether at the local level or in the leadership of the organisation, did not need the problems of mixed clubs spelt out to them, their everyday lived experience told them already. The NFWI in 1925 was an organisation of a quarter of a million women who consciously decided to govern themselves, without male interference or assistance, at a point when women had still not got the vote on equal terms with men. It may not seem a very significantly feminist organisation but feminism is about challenging the socially constructed role of women and the WI certainly enabled women to do just that. In 1923 Blake's 'Jerusalem' was adopted as the movement's song to be sung at all meetings. NFWI mythology claims it was chosen by Grace Hadow in reaction to the numerous alternative songs written by members. It is likely that its appeal lay in it having been used by the National Union of Suffrage Societies in the 1918 celebrations of women's enfranchisement[25] and is an indication of the Women's Institute Movement's links with the wider women's movement.

The NFWI was by no means the only women's organisation in the post-suffrage era. Its specificity was in its focus on rural women and its determination to be free of party political or religious denominational loyalties. It aimed at being open to all rural women unlike, for example, the Mothers' Union, which preceded it by a number of years, and was firmly rooted within the Church of England. Indeed the Mother's Union may have perceived the Women's Institute Movement as a threat to recruitment and this could explain the antagonism that there was in some areas towards WIs by the Church of England. C.A. Kingsmill, the first honorary secretary to the Hampshire Federation, recalled:

> Objections were often raised by those who said that WIs would be a dangerous rival to the Mothers' Union. Here I was greatly helped by the fact that my mother was at that time the Winchester Diocesan president of the MU. She was amused when people commiserated with her on the fact that her daughter was working for a rival organisation. She said the aims and objections were different and she saw no reason for a clash.[26]

Certainly organisations like the Mothers' Union and the Primrose League with their very specific religious or party allegiances had a very clear intention behind their recruitment of the working class. The presence of such vested interests amongst those who organised social events in rural villages at the turn of the century, is explained by one member of a newly formed WI who was heard to remark upon the uniqueness of arrangements – 'This is the first organisation I have been able to join in the village, ... everything else is got up by the Church and the Conservatives and I'm a Catholic and a Liberal'.[27] In attempting to bring together rural women across religious, class, and party lines there was an awareness of the potential for conflict. A significant rule in the very early days of the Women's Institute Movement, aimed at preventing any controversy, was that nothing which 'might cause friction or lead to serious differences' should be discussed and that the institutes must be non-sectarian and non-political. This ruling is indicative of the insecurity of the fledgling organisation but it also had very practical purposes in uniting women around the common bond of womanhood rather than around religion or male-defined political parties. The women involved in the movement came from the political left and right. Lloyd George's wife and daughter were involved in the higher levels of the organisation, William Morris's daughter May was, in the last years of her life, to act as secretary to her local WI and Neville Chamberlain's sister was also involved in the NFWI. Interestingly, condemnation of the organisation at one time or another came from both the political left and right. Once the NFWI were on their way to real independence an AGM resolution of 1918 followed which welcomed both controversial and political issues providing they could not be described as party political. This opened the doors to many of the campaigns, issues and concerns that I shall describe in latter chapters. What was termed party political remained an issue of controversy and contestation for some time. Their links with, and support of, the League of Nations Union for example, was not accepted as a suitable subject by many members.

The movement was specifically aimed at rural villages classified as no more than five thousand inhabitants, although an AGM resolution in 1920 allowed institutes to be set up in any mining village which was essentially 'rural in character'. This was at first merely significant as a guide for the hierarchy of the organisation concerning where to focus their efforts. Following the formation of the Townswomen's Guild in 1928 (with the advice and support of the NFWI), this became a more complex issue. It became from then on a ruling which was a demarcation guide between the two organisations. At a superficial level the organisations may not seem significantly different but this would be a misconception. Formed from the National Society for Equal Citizenship, the TWG had a ruling which forbade the discussion of anything which was likely to cause controversy. Furthermore, the demarcation issue became at times more heated as the differences between the organisations became more marked and as villages grew in size. In the 1950s particularly, this was to cause some friction but the five thousand ruling was not repealed until the 1980s.

However, I argued in the last chapter that it is absolutely vital to see feminist organisations in terms of networks. Belonging to one woman's organisation or another, very probably in the past, as today, was more concerned with convenience, what friends did and the interests of a specific point in women's lives rather than ideological purity. Some women saw the Women's Institute Movement as a natural continuance to their suffrage work and indeed the National Union of Women's Suffrage Societies was represented in the movement by Mrs Auerbach who was treasurer of the NUWSS and of the NFWI, as well as by Grace Hadow who was an Oxford don, a suffragist and for many years NFWI Vice Chairman, whereas the Women's Social and Political Union were represented iconographically by the NFWI's adoption of the green, purple and white colours of the WSPU for their banner. Women in the 1920s and 1930s created a sort of web between different women's organisations. Elizabeth

Robins, suffragette writer and author of the play *Votes for Women* which raised money for the suffrage cause, became a founder and President of her local East Sussex WI and remained so for most of the rest of her life. She also contributed to *Home and Country* magazine and more well known feminist publications like *Time and Tide* and wrote a feminist tract – *Ancilla's Share*.[28] The NFWI was linked to almost every other significant feminist campaign or organisation, between the two world wars, either in terms of personnel or through joint endeavours. A representative of the National Society for Equal Citizenship (the organisation which evolved from the NUWSS when women over thirty received the vote in 1918) spoke to the 1931 NFWI AGM in answer to a resolution about the disinheritance of wives and children. NUWSS and the Six Points Group promoted their activities and wrote about their concerns in *Home and Country*. Women from both these organisations and the Fabian Women's Group were involved in the WI.[29] The mother of the editor of *Time and Tide*, the Countess of Rhondda, was involved in the Welsh WI and wrote about the Six Point group for *Home and Country*. E.M. Delafield was another writer who wrote for these publications and was heavily involved in her local WI. Her *Diary of a Provincial Lady*, first published in parts in *Time and Tide*, frequently charts her WI involvement with a high level of wit.[30]

The NFWI were keen not to limit their networks only to predominantly middle-class organisations. They aimed to be a cross-class organisation and indeed many within the organisation saw their role as in some respects class conciliatory – a potentially important step in breaking down class antagonism. An East Sussex VCO's diary from East Sussex notes with disapproval any WI which does not include sufficient numbers of 'Cottage People'.[31] In the early days, the NFWI attempted to co-opt representatives of the Trade Union Movement on to the National Executive. In 1919 this was Lady Cowan representing the National Council of Women Workers. This was very probably a response to criticisms of the movement in *The Landworker*[32]. In 1922, Mrs Simms of the National Federation of General Workers was co-opted. In 1924 Mrs Simms place on the NFWI executive was in her own right to keep the federation in touch with the union point of view. It is interesting to note in support of this that at the 1927 AGM, Mrs Auerbach as honorary treasurer told the Institutes that – 'it must be regarded as a moral obligation on the county associations to set up a standard of good salaries for those who worked for them'.[33]

Furthermore the NFWI's National Federation Chairwoman Lady

Denman was also Chairperson of the Birth Control Council and later of the Family Planning Association which, like the NFWI, benefited from her financial resources. She was not the only person to belong to both groups. However birth control was never promoted directly by the NFWI in order not to break their constitution which ensured that all denominations would feel able to be members. It would have antagonised Catholics (as the Women's Co-op Guild discovered.[34] There were though, very definite links between the two organisations in terms of personnel and this was well known within the movement. In the immediate post-war years the NFWI campaigned on a whole variety of women's issues, sometimes with other organisations and sometimes on their own. *Home and Country*, the NFWI monthly magazine, attempted to raise women's interest in politics – which it explained in the 1920s as housekeeping on a larger scale. They ran a series of articles entitled 'Voters Awake' explaining the electoral and governmental system at local and national levels. Members were encouraged to partake at all points in the electoral process as voters, council and parliamentary representatives, whatever party they represented. It was argued that the women's point of view was needed in the political decision-making process. In 1921 an AGM resolution advised:

> That it be the recognised duty of individual institutes to educate their members in the powers of the Parish Councils, Rural District Councils and County Councils with a view to getting local women on all these bodies.[35]

Up until the 1950s, *Home and Country* included monthly reviews of any bills before Parliament which it was thought affected women. A public questions service was provided by the NFWI headquarters until the 1940s producing leaflets which provided information for the institutes in order to stimulate discussion. Thus the NFWI in attempting to politicise women and through links with a variety of other organisations raised the consciousness of rural women. It was able to operate at times as a springboard for women into other feminist and social welfare campaigns. However, they were not just limited to internal domestic politics.

They worked with the National Council of Women to promote the widespread introduction of women police.[36] They campaigned at national, county and village level for anything which was considered to improve the quality of rural women's lives. This obviously included much social welfare legislation, improvements in maternity provision, for example, where they worked with the League for Health, the Maternity and Child Welfare League, the National Baby Week Council and the National Council for Unmarried Mothers. Their campaigns for improvements in rural water, electricity and sewage facilities and more and better rural council housing are discussed in a later chapter. Their political activity also included more mundane and village-centred concerns, such as trying to prevent local bus companies raising the fare to the local market town – one of Chidham in West Sussex's more successful campaigns.

The NFWI, like many women's organisations in the period, was concerned with peace issues. They strongly promoted the League of Nations Union (LNU) – which both Winifred Holtby and Vera Brittain lectured for in 1919. A NFWI representative was appointed to the women's committee of the union and in time over six hundred Institutes were study associates of the LNU In 1931 the Women's League for Peace and Freedom attended the NFWI AGM to collect support and signatures for their disarmament petition and found it a worthwhile exercise. In 1934 the AGM passed the following resolution:

> We desire to reaffirm our faith in the League of Nations Union and to urge His Majesty's Government to do their utmost to secure a real measure of world disarmament; and further, we authorise co-operation where advisory between the NFWI and other organisations with a view to every possible effort being made to attain to this end. Further, we recommend that all Women's Institutes should endeavour during the next year to introduce into their programme something that would interest their members in the activities and outlook of other nations.[37]

And later that year a NFWI committee member, Miss Tennant, spoke at a peace demonstration held in Brussels and with over three hundred delegates from twenty countries.[38] The NFWI also had links with rural women's organisations in other countries.

Following her significant role in the formation of the Women's Institute Movement in Britain, Mrs Watt turned her attention to an attempt to form some sort of international organisation of rural women. Early attempts in the 1920s met with little success as a federal structure between organisations, some of which were independent of their governments and some of which were not, was impractical. The NFWI instead affiliated itself to the International Congress of Agriculture as a way of ensuring informal links between and meetings of rural women. Mrs Watt, however, remained determined and was instrumental in the setting up of the International Council of Women which held a conference in 1929 for representatives of rural women's organisations. This resulted in the formation of a joint standing committee and in 1933 the Associated Countrywomen of the World (ACWW) emerged with Mrs Watt as its first President. The NFWI remained uncertain about the organisation and did not affiliate until 1935. Some of this hesitancy can certainly be ascribed to the views of Lady Denman. The ACWW held conferences every three years and in 1939, in London, the arrival there of the German delegates was greeted with widespread applause; the audience presumably pleased that the communality of rural women transcended national antagonisms. The ACWW also organised a variety of competitions, contacts and exchange visits between different rural women, particularly in the post-war period, when their offices were in London.

Early promoters of the Women's Institute Movement perceived it to have a role in rejuvenating rural areas, attributed perhaps to the Victorian ideal of women as moral guardians of the nation[39] and the late nineteenth- and early twentieth-century resurgence of 'back-to the-landism' (the idea, strong within British culture, that there is something intrinsically and unarguably better about the rural way of life). Following the crisis of the 1880s, with high unemployment, resultant political unrest and deep concern about the perceived moral and physical degeneration of the urban working class particularly in the light of *Bitter Cry of Outcast London*,[40] attention turned to rural England as far preferable to some of the worst excesses of industrial capitalism. A concern over population shifts to the towns was shared by a wide variety of people of all shades of the political spectrum. The writings of Rider Haggard were one example, also George Lansbury's hopes that labour colonies could provide a potential retraining in the skills required of agricultural labourers for the urban working class of Poplar. During the war period the Women's Institute Movement perceived themselves as helping to feed the nation through their efforts to improve food production. It also hoped to feed the nation morally through the rejuvenation of the rural areas. Behind the war was a perception, however illusory, of defence of country, home and family. To many at the front, or perhaps more importantly, in the home front, the perception of the England that they were fighting for was rural. It was an England of Helen Allingham pictures and of postcards of home depicting villages, farms and country cottages. It was not necessarily the rural life of pre-war England that was depicted, rather it was an improved and reworked version.

The rhetoric of an improved post-war version of England and of Englishness became second nature to WI speakers. They spoke of a perception of village life and rural womanhood's place in it, along with notions of co-operation, service and class conciliation rather than that of confrontation and exploitation which may have been a more familiar perception to many of their listeners. The WI was seen, by some involved in it, as a significant part of post-war reconstruction and thus they developed a perception of post-war ruralism within which 'villagism' was paramount. The WI was to have a crucial role to play in revitalising the villages, to stem the perceived population flood from the land to the towns. Mrs Huddart, when speaking in 1917, said upon the matter, 'Women's Institutes, by presenting so many and varied things to women in the country, will do more than anything to keep them in these better and healthier surroundings'.[41] The NFWI's own perception of 'Jerusalem' in this period and the 1920s relied on a reconstructed rural past and an almost visionary perception of the future and was therefore able to gain ready acceptance, especially as it drew on wartime rhetoric. Within this context, of wartime, the potential rejuvenation of rural life by the WI laid stress on two particular realisable elements – agriculture or food production and community service. WI women spoke of duty and patriotism. Mrs Watt, for example, in 1917 encouraged all members to ask 'What is my home, my garden, my farm doing for my Country?'[42] Indeed in this quote and her early speeches, there is an indication of Mrs Watt's perception of the Women's Institutes as predominantly concerned with food production. The organisations which funded the WIs formation were agricultural and consequently it is not surprising that food production and agriculture, particularly within wartime, were significant elements in the formative years of the Movement. It was not necessarily agricultural work on farms for women which was encouraged, but more often a sort of cottage farming. The suggested audience for the publicity poster of the inaugural meeting, of what was to be the first WI in England, at Singleton issued a special invitation to 'holders of cottage gardens and village allotments'.[43]

Demonstrations and talks were provided within the monthly

meetings on subjects such as: rabbit- and pig-keeping, gardening, cheese making, rabbit skin curing, herb collecting and goat husbandry. The sales tables provided the opportunity to sell excess produce. Some areas even had clubs devoted to pig- or goat-keeping. To many rural women poultry-keeping had traditionally been a significant source of independent income and in the early days this was an area in which the membership seemed to have an interest. The NFWI were quick to become a member of the National Poultry Council seeing their role, as representing the interests of the smallholder, as important. However by 1928 they withdrew as they felt that they could not claim it to be an interest of many of the members anymore.

Agriculture was not to retain a significant role within the WI beyond the early 1920s although the World War Two again brought about an emphasis on food production. Agricultural concerns had two strands – concern with the training and wages of those women who worked in the industry and encouragement of members to be productive within their cottage gardens and allotments. Maybe in this second area of cottage garden and allotment production they were not taking into consideration the complexity of gender divisions around food production. Allotments and vegetable growing tended to be perceived as male spheres and were not necessarily ones women wanted to take on. If divisions of domestic labour are an area of contestation and a site of power struggle, many women may see an attempt to take over one of the few areas of household labour which men did undertake as offering little advantage. The superwoman of the 1990s who does all the traditional female roles within the household and many other domestic tasks once considered a male preserve is possibly doing little to break down sexism. Arguably she is just proving true the dictum that feminism would liberate men before it liberated women. The women in the first WIs who seemed reluctant to take over traditionally male tasks should be seen in the light of this experience.

Alternatively, others who either did not live with men or whose men were absent or unreliable might perceive cottage farming as a source of independence and power. Some women who had trained as gardeners saw the movement as a space in which to use and develop their skills and expertise. Miss Margaret Rotherham who was involved in the WI leadership at county and national levels in the period before and after the World War Two and in the formation of Denman College recalls:

I had always been mad on gardening and I wished to go to Horticultural

College. So I went to Studley and was there two years and learned an awful lot. I was happy there, and I got the Horticultural Certificate of the RHS. I think that going to Studley has been the background to all I have done. I have always been doing either gardening or fruit preservation or something along those lines.[44]

County Councils were often eager to provide financial aid towards WI classes oriented towards agriculture and horticulture and in 1927 the extra mural department of Leeds University provided local institutes with classes in dairying. Some of these achieved real success. The same cannot be said for the residential courses planned for WI members only in 1924 and 1925. Organised by the Agriculture and Horticulture sub-committee of the NFWI they were on dairy work, horticulture and poultry and held at Seale Hayne Agricultural College in Devon and the Herefordshire Institute for Agriculture and Horticulture. In 1924 attendance was eleven and four respectively and in 1925 the courses had to be cancelled. Maybe those who would have been interested were unable to attend a residential course. At least the courses were oriented towards a perception of WI members as agricultural workers and, consistent with this, the WI constantly petitioned for women's interests to be represented on the Agricultural Wages Board. In 1926 an attempt was made to counteract the male bias of such boards when the NFWI requested of the Board of Agriculture that at least one of the independent members on Wages Boards should be a woman; by 1930 they were demanding that the Government Land Settlement Schemes should be available to women in their own right. If there is a general feeling now amongst historians that agricultural work for women was inevitably fading away in this period, it was not ncessarily a view shared by the NFWI.

Concern over the importance of agriculture to the Institutes was clear in an article in *Home and Country* in 1930 which saw agriculture as unable to 'compete with handicrafts, music or drama in providing occupation for the long winter evenings' but still urged county federations to give it more time and energy than it was getting. There was great stress laid on the role of the smallholder's wife and it was argued that:

Women excel in certain branches of work such as dairying, poultry, young livestock and, in the Fens and other parts of the country, in much seasonal work. One fifth of the workers in Agriculture and Horticulture are women and there is an increase in the number of dairy herd owners.[45]

Although some would disagree over the significance of women in agriculture at this time, the leadership of the NFWI can be seen to still encourage their participation through the pages of *Home and Country* to still encourage it. In all probability they were swimming against the tide of working-class women's own requirements. Agricultural work was both physically hard and low paid and many working-class women, in the 1920s, may have found domesticity, if affordable, much more desirable. If the idea of rejuvenating rural areas through the Women's Institute's involvement in agriculture and food production was not an unquestionable success, then community service perhaps was.

In wartime notions of nationhood are obviously very important. War becomes totally farcical without a strongly developed idea of the cohesion of a nation and some perception, however illusory, of the difference between one nation and another. Such perceptions of nationhood are often developed first from a sense of identification with family and community. Thus, as the Women's Institute Movement developed in wartime it frequently adopted a rhetoric of community service which was perceived as part of the national war effort. The 1926 annual report noted:

> As the Institutes strengthen and consolidate their own organisation, their ability to render really effective community service is naturally increased. It is significant that when the Institute movement was started, during the war, it owed much of its success to the fact that it gave every country woman the opportunity to take part in work for public good.... and this is still a side of their work that Institutes can not afford to neglect.[46]

The idea of community service was to remain an integral part of the movement's ideology, and was still in evidence in the Keep Britain Tidy Campaign of the 1950s although its importance varied enormously. In 1931 the Anglesey Federation reported the different forms and consequent meanings that community service could have within the movement:

> Many Institutes take an active interest in the children of the village. One has, in co-operation with the school managers, formulated a scheme for helping necessitous children by providing clothing, boots, etc., in the

35

winter. Christmas parties have been given in several villages for the school children. Clinics have been run in co- operation with the district nursing associations. Model outfits for infants have been made, under the direction of the Superintendent of nursing for North Wales. Local hospitals and village halls have been generously helped.[47]

It could be argued that voluntary organisations like the NFWI plugged gaps in state and local government provision for the needy, thereby consequently ameliorating potential crisis in dominant hegemonies. But their role is much more complex than this, they may have provided an area within which the role of the state, and mass consent to it, could be questioned and contested. Women play a unique role within this mixed economy of welfare being both significant providers to plug gaps in state provision, and consumers. Their need for welfare is heightened as much by certain times in their lives when, for example, they have small children, as by class. Within the context of rural villages, an organisation taking on a paternalistic role (which was previously undertaken by the gentry) may alter the power relationships involved. There is a greater variety of meanings, or readings, of the organisation of a soup kitchen, or the loan of a layette (both schemes some WIs were running in 1918) if it is run by an organisation with an ideological, at least, commitment to democracy than if it is run by or funded by an individual. This is particularly so if many of the beneficiaries of some of the community services are members of the organisation themselves – then it becomes an empowering self-help group. Furthermore if the organisation is made up of women, who are perceived as at least one step removed from the capitalist process, which has brought about the necessity for the soup kitchen or other forms of welfare, then the scope for different meanings and potential empowerment for women exists in such schemes.

Another significant area of community service was in relation to unemployment and the distressed mining areas in the 1920s. NFWI experts were called upon to teach handicrafts in unemployment retraining centres, although the 1934 Annual Report records that this was only a short term project which had been taken over by the National Council for Social Services. The NFWI co-operated with the Society of Friends in the provision of seeds and tools for the unemployed to work on allotments in 1934, as well as attempting to help relocate miners and other unemployed men and their families.

This could be seen as a new form of paternalism from the rural south, in particular, to the depressed industrial areas. It could also be a system for the flow of information presenting different perceptions of the meaning of the Depression to the south. The sending of parcels of clothes to distressed mining areas, as Funtington in West Sussex did in the 1920s, was one form of practical welfare provision engaged in by institutes. In 1936 *Home and Country* had a short story called 'The Christmas Parcel', illuminating the positive advantages brought to a southern institute and a Jarrow family when a WI sent the family of an unemployed man a Christmas parcel containing clothes, a Christmas cake and presents for the children. The arrangements were made between the institute and the Jarrow mother. The tricky issue of charity is dealt with when Clara in Jarrow receives the letter offering help:

> Clara put down the letter. She had never accepted charity, nor had any of her people. Could she take this parcel? Yet was it 'charity'? They said it would give them pleasure. She read the letter over again; it was all so friendly, just as if those people in Dorset understood what she had been feeling. No doubt they had their troubles, who has not? Yes she would let them send the parcel.[48]

Within this story the emphasis is on mutuality and women helping each other, at a specific point in their lives when they have problems, without the power relationship that patronage and paternalism entails. The story ends on the joy brought to a Dorset WI member, who cannot have children, as on Christmas morning she thinks of the girl in Jarrow who will receive the doll she had bought and dressed. Potentially there are different meanings and interpretations in such a story, as in the whole issue of community service. It could provide the first steps towards social welfare demands, it could be an example of nineteenth-century paternalism and, at the very least, it would alert rural women to the very different material circumstances in which other women were living.

Many institute activities, which came under the heading of community service, were in some way related to provision of health services prior to the founding of the NHS, for example, collecting farm eggs for local hospitals, running infant welfare clinics, funding a district nurse and buying the local midwife the necessary equipment to administer analgesics to women in childbirth. These activities could bring to the women involved in the movement, an awareness that the individual could not meet all their needs themselves and needed some external help. Arguably, it is not a large step from the notion that an organisation or group should provide such services, to the argument that the state should. Certainly these welfare activities encompassed within them a challenge to any remnants of Victorian self-help and individualist ideology. It is interesting that the emphasis on community service within the NFWI in the post-war period operated alongside moves to embrace demands for social welfare legislation, the following 1926 AGM resolution indicates this requesting – 'that this meeting urges all Women's Institutes to study the different methods of National Health and other Insurance, in the interests of members and the families of members'.[49]

By the mid-1920s the Women's Institute Movement was established as an independent organisation which had affirmed its focus as rural, primarily domestic women and in whose interests it was prepared to be both controversial and political. It had established links with many of the significant feminist organisations of the period. The organisation was broadening out from its principally agricultural base and developing notions of community service into demands for social welfare legislation. For rural domestic women it had carved out a significant space which was able to be developed in both cultural and social terms and as a potential instrument of political representation. An indication of the perception of the leadership of NFWI's need to solidify their sense of identity can be seen in the writing of the first NFWI history in 1925 and so it is the changing perceptions of the movement as expressed in histories to which the next chapter will turn. This will provide something of an overview of the movement. Although the structure of the organisation changed little from the early period, the priorities and concerns of the movement did. It can be seen from this chapter how issues and central concerns of the Movement in one historical period lose their significance over time as agriculture and food production did. It can also be difficult to keep within neat time bands in looking at themes like community service which was, to a more limited degree, still of relevance in the 1950s. The format of exploring the histories followed by the next chapters looking at how the organi-sation's concerns developed in specific periods of time, interspersed with case studies, is an attempt to deal with this problem. I hope that what will emerge is a sense of how, from the basis developed in the first ten years, the NFWI provided many women with a space to develop themselves as women often beyond social and cultural expectations and thus became the 'acceptable face of feminism'.

NOTES

1. Inez Jenkins, *The History of the Women's Institute Movement in England Wales*, Oxford University Press, Oxford 1953, p77.
2. J.W. Robertson Scott, *The Story of the Women's Institute Movement*, Virago Press, Idbury 1925, Chapter Two.
3. *ibid*. p22.
4. *ibid*. p29.
5. *ibid*. p43.
6. *Home and Country*, October 1925, p27.
7. J.W. Robertson Scott, *op cit*., p54.
8. Pioneer ideology relating to women is explored in J.R. Jeffrey, *Frontier Women*, Hill and Wang, New York 1979.
9. J.W. Robertson Scott, *op cit*., p151.
10. Lady Oliver, *Jubilee Book*, NFWI publication, London 1965.
11. J.W. Robertson Scott, *op cit*., p49.
12. Archive File in NFWI archive.
13. Gervas Huxley, *Lady Denman*, Chatto and Windus, Oxford 1961, describes in a fairly reserved way her private life as well as her more public activities.
14. Inez Jenkins, *op cit*., p18.
15. Catherine Blair, *Rural Journey*, Nelson, London 1940, describes the formation of the Scottish equivilent of the NFWI.
16. *Western Morning News*, 15 June 1927.
17. Mrs Alfred Watt and N. Lloyd, *The First Women's Institute School*, NFWI publication, London 1918.
18. *ibid*. p131.
19. History File in NFWI archive.
20. Inez Jenkins, *op cit*., p31.
21. *ibid*., p47.
22. J.W. Robertson Scott, *op cit*., p134.
23. *ibid*. p134.
24. *Home and Country*, July 1923, p17.
25. Anne Oakley, 'Millicent Garett Fawcett – Duty and Determination', in D. Spender (ed.), *Feminist Theorists*, Virago, London 1983, p195.
26. Oral Testimony (5) typed and kept in archive file in NFWI archive, p4.
27. Lady Oliver, *op cit*., p6.
28. Elizabeth Robins, *Ancilla's Share*, 1924 reprint, Hutchinson, London 1976, for a more detailed analysis of her activities, J. Alberti, *Beyond the Suffrage*, Macmillan, London 1989.
29. The six points of the so named group were –
    1] Satisfactory legislation on child assault.
    2] Satisfactory legislation for widowed mothers.

3] Satisfactory legislation for the unmarried mother and her child.
4] Equal guardianship.
5] Equal pay for men and women teachers.
6] Equal pay for men and women in the cival service.
30. E.M. Delafield, *Diary of a Provincial Lady*, London 1930, reprinted Virago, London 1984, also see D. Spender, *Time and Tide Wait For No Man*, Pandora, London 1984.
31. VCO's diary held in East Sussex Federation of Women's Institutes Archive.
32. *The Landworker*, October 1919).
33. *Home and Country*, July 1927, p277.
34. For a more detailed study of the Women's Co-operative Guild see G. Scott, 'The Working Class Women's Most Assertive and Democratic Movement 1883–1952', unpublished D.Phil thesis (Sussex 1988).
35. Mrs Neve Scarborough, *History of the Associated Countrywomen of the World*, Collins, London 1953.
36. Edith Tancred, *Women Police*, London 1950.
37. *Keeping Ourselves Informed*, NFWI publication, London 1981, p82.
38. Inez Jenkins, *op cit.*, p131.
39. C. Hall, 'The Early Formation of Victorian Domestic Ideology', in S. Burman (ed.), *Fit Work for Women*, Croom Helm, London 1979.
40. G. Stedman Jones, *Outcast London*, Clarendon, Oxford 1971.
41. Mrs Alfred Watt, *op cit.*, p43.
42. *ibid.* p42.
43. Singleton WI History, held by Singleton WI.
44. Miss Walters, oral testimony (7) typed and kept in History file in NFWI archive.
45. *Home and Country*, May 1930, p197.
46. 1926 NFWI annual report, p9.
47. 1931 NFWI annual report, p73.
48. *Home and Country*, 1936, p697.
49. 1926 NFWI annual report, p46.

3

IDENTITY PROBLEMS

– A HISTORY OF THE HISTORIES –

As I have explained in the last chapter, by the mid-1920s the NFWI was securely established as an independent and democratic self-financing organisation. By 1925 it had a quarter of a million members. The leadership began to consolidate their position, to solidify the emerging sense of identity the movement was beginning to establish and in the same year the first history of the Women's Institute Movement was written. If, as I argued in chapter one, producing a history serves a political purpose in terms of constructing a national culture, then it certainly does the same for the internal politics of an organisation. The various histories of the movement, predominantly written with NFWI co-operation if not sponsorship, are an illuminating insight into dominant views of the organisation at particular stages in its history. The very writing of a history by an organisation is often a consolidating and validating action. It may well take place at a point of crisis or change and may be a significant attempt to create within the movement a sense of unity and thus it can become an assertion of a sense of consciousness or identity. The 'our glorious past' of an organisation's history is far more a case of one version of 'our glorious present and future'. The identity of the NFWI as presented within these histories (written in almost every decade) fed into the discourse within the organisation and framed how the membership of the movement was perceived as a lived experience by its members. The histories therefore are about how the Women's Institute Movement perceived and constituted themselves as a group or a community. In order to do this, like any other group, they drew boundaries of inclusion and exclusion in relation to activities, ideologies, political views and involvement, which served to produce a particular definition of the NFWI and its membership. This definition was not static but changing and constantly the site of renegotiation over time. Indeed, the histories are part of these renegotiations. However, the histories are themselves also part of the NFWI's attempt to belong to other groups, specifically those perceived to be – the nation or maybe more precisely – 'the English' and of 'the women's movement'. Stuart Hall has argued that at any one time those who are perceived to be genuinely included within definitions of the nation is very small; the majority of the population is excluded.[1] Amongst the excluded there are subalterns who are perceived as included, but only conditionally and with a second class status. From a perspective of socialist feminist historiography I want to argue that the position of women as subalterns is always conditional.

The NFWI's rural domestic base meant that they were in a sense able to tap into a notion of Englishness which encompassed the rural village and the rural home as the heart of England. But within such an idea of Englishness the perceptions of rural womanhood which gained cultural currency were domestic but also maternal, passive and accepting. Jane Mackay and Pat Thane have argued that at the turn of the century 'an image of the Englishwoman was strangely elusive' but it was believed to be universal.[2] They argue that this role of the Englishwoman became elevated to national importance. Thus:

> Domestic harmony created, and sustained, by women was presented as desirable, even essential, for the defence of Britain against her rivals overseas, indeed the defence of the whole British Empire. It was a role demanded of women of all social classes, since healthy soldiers and workers were vital for national survival as businessmen and officers.[3]

This perception of women is almost diametrically opposed to that commonly taken as signified by the other group that the NFWI identified with – the Women's Movement and feminism. Englishness has consistently defined itself in such a way that feminism is positively excluded.

Women are constantly struggling over the terms and conditions of their acceptance as part of the nation. For women in the NFWI their ruralism enabled them to be included in definitions of the nation and, indeed, at times to be perceived as the epitome of Englishness, despite their feminism. However, the movement never really aligned itself with overt feminism or wished to be included in a definition of the feminist movement as this would have threatened their conditional inclusion in a sense of Englishness. Thus, I would want to argue that the NFWI demonstrates the acceptable face of feminism; struggling over the economic, political and cultural position of women but within the space allowed them by the dominant power blocs. I shall therefore examine previous histories of the NFWI within the framework of defining those included and excluded by the movement and its consequent sense of identity, their role in the efforts of the Women's Institute Movement in trying to establish itself as included within both the nation and the women's movement. The NFWI histories at one level chart the changes over the conditions upon which they are included as part of the nation; they are also part of the struggles over those conditions. In summary I argue that this moves from a version of post-suffrage ruralism in the 1920s, through the inclusion of a form of political combination in the 1930s, to a radical version of social welfare capitalism in the war period. In the 1950s there appears to be a regressive shift to a domestic and apolitical version of the NFWI.

The first history of the NFWI written in 1925 was J.W. Robertson Scott's *The Story of the Women's Institute Movement in England and Wales*.[4] Predictably it embodied many of the concerns and themes of the movement at the time – the ruralism, a notion of Englishness and a concern over the significance of the NFWI as a women-only organisation and its relationship to feminism. Obviously at such an early stage in the movement's development the book was about publicising and justifying the Women's Institute Movement to outsiders especially in relation to the government grants the NFWI had received during the war period. Much of the book is spent describing the activities of the movement and portraying the WI's in terms of their rural and domestic base and their encouragement of a politically active, autonomous womanhood. With these concerns to the fore the history attempts to create a sense of the NFWI as unified though complex and varied, validated by a sense of its past and a tradition. The writing of a history was thus an act of consolidation for the movement. The book traces the foundation and establishment of Women's Institutes in Canada, England, Wales and Scotland. The move from the original sponsorship by the AOS to the Board of Agriculture and finally to independence is described in some detail as is the establishment of the Women's Institute Movement originally in Canada, the first WI in Britain (which was in Wales) and the separate development of the Scottish Rurals. The book relies heavily on personal testimonies and anecdotes; the movement is essentially perceived as made up of individuals and events. A further book *The Women's Institutes at Work and Play: A tour of investigation, with thoughts about the future by the best minds of the Movement* by the same author was planned but never came to be published.

J.W. Robertson Scott was by politics a liberal, pro-ruralism and pro-women's suffrage; not too distant ideologically from Lady Denman, the first NFWI chairwoman. The two ideological debts of the organisation – to the women's movement and to ruralism – are acknowledged. The early chapters and introduction to the book are imbued with notions of rejuvenating village life and the NFWI as a continuum at some level with the feminism of the suffrage movements. The rural question and the need to revitalise the villages in order to preserve a rural version of Englishness was a preoccupation of members of all political parties at the time. Robertson Scott was able to marry this with a legacy of the suffrage campaigns within the NFWI because he was writing in 1925 after women over thirty had been enfranchised. When a radical or feminist demand becomes accepted and part of the legal structure then some of those who fought for it can be redefined as part of the nation rather than excluded. Emmeline Pankhurst went from being regarded as a criminal to having her statue outside the Houses of Parliament. Thus by 1925 it was possible to redefine support for the suffrage within a version of Englishness. The alignment to the women's movement is described in a slightly paternalistic, possibly patronising style thus – 'This book records, happily, not only the growth of the Women's Institute Movement, but the growth of women'.[5] Or alternatively the book is described as:

> a truthful narrative of the experiences of this remarkable women's movement which is of social and political value.
>
> 1. It shows how countrywomen are now, like townswomen, working out their own salvation technically, socially, and in the best sense of the word politically.
>
> 2. It makes plain some of the better methods of rural advance, for men as well as women, if we are going to have any worthy agricultural life at all.[6]

Scott clearly saw, in my view correctly, the NFWI as an organisation for the improvement of both the material circumstances of women's lives and perhaps more significantly of their self-confidence and assertiveness. Although Scott places emphasis on personalities in the instigation of the movement, there is also space given to the importance of war conditions and the suffrage movement. Thus he argues:

> The institutes came at the culmination of the agitation for the suffrage, that is at a time when a great deal has been done in educating women for working together.... 'The suffragists made the pot to boil' Mr Harris said to me; 'The WI showed how some things could be got out of the pot'.[7]

Thus the continuum between the suffrage movement and the NFWI, which I would argue is an important notion for the analysis of the movement, was recognised at the time; however in terms of the discourse within which the book is written, it is a connection which Scott is hesitant about emphasising. The book is very conscious of the significance of the NFWI as an all-women organisation. It is very defensive about this, constantly trying to tread a path between justifying the need for women to create their own spaces and attempting to keep some sense of distance between the NFWI and more overtly feminist organisations. This, I think, is about preventing the movement being tarred with a feminist brush and the consequent alienation that this would cause both to members and potential members. Indeed, this is a tension within the text and the movement because an overt identification with feminism would in all probability have rendered the NFWI excluded from definitions of Englishness.

These concerns were very much the preoccupation of the movement, having as recently as 1923 voted to exclude men from any sort of membership and having consciously decided that the movement had to be quite separate from the Village Clubs Association, which in the early 1920s had made moves to suggest an amalgamation. Certainly an amalgamation would have been negative in financial terms for the NFWI. The early demise of the VCA seeming to be proof of this. As Scott argues:

> If the appearance of the VCA had less of the appearance of a middle-aged young man with an uncertain future sidling up to a prosperous young woman with a big establishment and an assured future, the wooers might have received a more cordial reception than was vouchsafed them.[8]

However the NFWI received some criticism of its rejection of the VCA. Sir Henry Rew accused the meeting of having a feminist atmosphere. Scott finds it necessary to defend their position as a women only organisation, saying for example – 'If the Federation leaders in their relations with the VCA were feminist, they were loyal to the countrywomen whose needs can only be met, for the present, by a woman 'organisation'.[9] That so much attention was placed on justifying the women-only nature of the organisation and this by a man, is really an indication of how much the NFWI – by its very existence – challenged the cultural definitions of female behaviour at this time.

Scott's history was published by The Village Press. In Robertson Scott's own words:

> This book has been written in the heart of the country as it should be, and it comes to its readers from a little publishing office which I have set up in a hamlet for the benefit of publishing not only this volume, but it may be, of other rural publications, by myself and other writers, which it is desired should be 'truly rural'.[10]

This extract embodies much that is intrinsic to NFWI thinking at the time and will be explored in future chapters – the elevation of the rural and the celebration of cottage industry in what I shall argue is an anti-capitalist form which owes a lot to William Morris. However, in the hands of Scott there was a fairly precise notion of how this ruralism should operate and how it could carry with it meanings and significances which offered more scope for the development of a consensus aligned to dominant definitions of good taste and culture than they did for personal development. For example:

> The handicrafts side of the movement suffers, as was to be expected in three ways. It suffers from the feeble pretentiousness of undisciplined women. It suffers from the precocity of women who have profited neither by George Bourne's *Wheelwrights Shop* nor Professor Lethabys's *Home and Country Arts* (which the movement has done well to publish), to learn that art was first of all concerned with the common things of daily life. It suffers from the eager inexperience of mothers of families who delight, in varying degrees, in the new world which craft work has opened to them, but have, naturally a dozen and one interests and duties, of the claimant demands of which better-off women will

have no more than a hazy notion. Many of these craftsmen in the cottages have neither the experience of study or the aptitude for it.[11]

This seems to dismiss notions of empowerment and autonomy and to be more about a definite attempt to inculcate rural working-class women with a particular line on craftwork. Whatever the debt to the arts and craft movement in these ideas, this was still somewhat questionable. It also indicates the inevitable failure of such attempts which I will explore in more detail in the next chapter. Scott does not despair. He perceives the movement, or at least its leaders, as working to 'regain the practice of home handicrafts with a view to restoring the best traditions of English workmanship'.[12]

As I have argued, a strand within both left- and right-wing thinking at the time expressed concern over the demise of rural England and held notions that within some sort of ruralism lay the solution to many of the worst excesses or failures of industrial capitalism brought to light from the latter part of the nineteenth century. Scott, in referring to Lethaby, is placing NFWI practice within this debate – Lethaby having been strongly influenced by and involved with William Morris. Indeed in the prologue Scott, referring to people who have moved into the countryside, claims:

> If our countryside means more to them than what they can get out of it for themselves, they come face to face with that condition-of-the-people-of-Britain question from which there is no escape on any acre of our rural or urban land.[13]

It is interesting that Scott addresses himself to those who have moved into the country, who are perceived as having the benefits of an urban culture in terms of broadened cultural and political horizons but who identify themselves with England's rural heartland, so to speak. The concern with rural England was not principally centred on agriculture, though the book does point out early WIs involvement with food production; rather it was perceived more in cultural and ideological terms and was linked to the population movement towards urban areas which was seen as a symptom of the cultural crisis of the rural areas. 'The institutes' Scott argues 'were to fill a permanent need in the rural life of the nation'.[14] The institutes were presented as able to offer a new social and cultural heart to the villages and one which would cross class lines. Thus Scott says, 'The movement must be agricultural and must be the cottage woman's movement as much or more than the countess's or it was nothing'.[15]

The book is dedicated to the youngest members of the movement and the memory of Mrs Hoodless. Mrs Hoodless was to become, with the help of Scott's book, the ideologically constructed founder of the Women's Institute Movement worldwide. She was an almost mythical figure who formed the first WI in Stoney Creek in Canada and according to the narrative, just an ordinary rural housewife whose youngest child died as a result of her own ignorance of food hygiene. Determined that such a tragedy should not happen to other women, she started the Women's Institute Movement. What better proof could there be of the necessity of educating women than the direct risk to the race and labour stock through ignorance? Women themselves were thus organising to improve their knowledge of domestic affairs. At one level this could be an empowering history or tradition for the movement, of women taking control of their own lives and co-operatively seeking knowledge and skills. That this version of events has but a passing relationship to any material reality is here irrelevant. Mrs Hoodless was but one of a number of people involved in the formation of the Women's Institutes, besides which Mrs Hoodless was involved in white collar work and, in social class terms, she was far from an ordinary rural housewife. Furthermore the Government always played a significant role in the formation of the Canadian institutes. However, folktales and myths are just that; they have their own truths, their own reality not fixed but open to interpretation. The NFWI perception of itself as an educational movement was open to two quite differing interpretations: either that of education as an instrument of bourgeois hegemony, the recipient of which was the ignorant rural housewife, or, alternatively education as empowering for the oppressed. Obviously, no situation is entirely one or the other but rather a struggle between the two, as was the meaning put upon the Mrs Hoodless story.

As the dedication suggests, Scott's NFWI history began in Canada in the 1890s, thus giving the movement a longer and more legitimising history, a longer tradition. This is despite huge differences in the movements which are not pointed out – the Canadian institutes never became the autonomous women's pressure group that the British organisation did. The links with the colonies are embedded with the pioneer spirit and therefore contain greater ideological distanciation from urban industrialisation. Many proponents of ruralism at the time, from all positions on the political spectrum, viewed a colonial existence as somehow more natural, more real, untainted by the worst excesses and alienation of industrial or consumer capitalism. The setting up of institutes in this country is strongly attributed by Scott to Mrs Watt. While not wanting to go over ground covered in the last chapter, it is interesting how her first meeting with Mr Nugent Harris is described:

> Mrs Watt went to the meeting and, Mr Harris told me, sat and knitted in the first row. Mr Harris says that, after he had spoken, Mrs Watt introduced herself to him. She told him she wanted to talk to him about Women's Institutes. His reply was 'but what are Women's Institutes?'[16]

The image of Mrs Watt sitting knitting within this formal predominantly male meeting is symbolic of the attempt to win female cultural space within a predominantly male culture, which the formation of the WI is in many respects all about. The story is placed centrally within the text and is typical of and consistent with a presentation of WI members by Scott both as assertive women yet with that assertiveness still grounded within a traditional, safe notion of domestic femininity.

The dedication's linking of a suitable past for the NFWI, using the story of Mrs Hoodless with the reference to new younger members is an attempt to put together a perception of the past with the author's (and many of the NFWI's national executive) hopes for the future. By 1925 there were a quarter of a million members nationwide, they were self-financing, independent of the Government and were established as both a cultural force within rural villages and a significant women's pressure group. The version of history that Robertson Scott presents explores the boundaries of the Women's Institutes. Their most significant exclusion was obviously men and consequently this issue receives much attention, but it is handled so as to ensure their inclusion within definitions of Englishness. This identification of their interests with those of the national interest was a position they were later to exploit for their own political purposes. In 1933 Janet Courtney published her version of the history of the NFWI. It was entitled *Countrywomen in Council – The English and Scottish Women's Institutes with chapters on the Movement in the dominions and the Townswomen's Guilds.*[17] It is by no means an official history but written by an outsider. Courtney had also written on the Women's Movement in the 1930s.[18] She includes in the introduction to

Countrywomen in Council the disclaimer – 'My book is written quite independently of the National Federation of Women's Institutes and no statement in it is authorised by them'.[19] Consequently Courtney's history differs very much from Robertson Scott's and the other histories looked at in this chapter as it does not represent the official leadership position but that of a quasi-outsider.

The tradition that Courtney creates for the NFWI is not colonial. It is rather a tradition purely of English ruralism. However, this is not the idyllic ruralism of some earlier writers. It is a ruralism based upon: oppression, poverty, struggle and the necessity for trade unions to combat this. In the introduction she explains her version of the formation of the NFWI thus: 'The remedy sought by the agricultural labourer in Arch's day is the remedy women were seeking when war broke over their heads – combination, co-operation strength in union'.[20] Drawing on the work of the Hammonds on the rural labourer in particular, Courtney talks at length about the exploitation of rural workers, the personal history of Joseph Arch, the history of agricultural workers' unions and women's previous failure to form combinations which she attributes to the problem of women rarely working together in large numbers.[21] It is interesting to note that the WIs had been on occasions criticised by agricultural workers' unions in the 1920s. One wonders how much the Courtney history is aimed at intervening in debate on the political implications for the left, and male trade unions in particular, of women organising independently of men and across class lines in rural villages. The importance of women as nineteenth-century agricultural workers is stressed in Courtney's book and their part in the Land Army of the World War One and also in cottage farming as encouraged through the NFWI. The institute's role in increasing wartime food production is also emphasised. The housewives who belong to the Women's Institutes are very much perceived by Courtney as skilled workers although unpaid and domestic. This is a theme which had much support in the institutes at the time, in some other areas of the feminist movement and also, to a certain extent, within the labour movement. Emphasis is also placed on the development of the NFWI as an independent self-financing organisation and its relationship with other women's organisations such as: the National Council of Women Workers, the National Council of Social Service and the Women's Local Government Society. The links with Women's Institutes and similar organisations in other countries and within the British Isles are an important part of the book and the NFWI is presented as very much part of a wider women's movement. However, the term women's movement cannot here be taken to be synonymous with a feminist movement.

The history also reviews the educational side of the movement: handicrafts, drama, singing, the contribution of the NFWI to the spread of libraries in rural areas and its involvement in rural community councils. A portrayal of the movement as diffuse is certainly part of the book but, as the title suggests, the NFWI is perceived as primarily a political movement and nowhere more so than in the chapter entitled 'A Parliament of Women'. The problem of women getting their interests represented and the NFWI's solution are explored. The following quote illuminates this well.

> They were to discover as many had expected that the vote was a double-edged weapon of limited usefulness, which cuts both ways. It involved them in the strife of parties, yet gave them only a very small percentage of representation in parliament. What they needed was just what the Institutes offered, a non-party all-embracing organisation in which the slow-speaking countrywoman, as much as her readier sisters, could make her voice heard. If the womanhood of the nation, irrespective of party, class, or creed could combine to bring their influence to bear upon the Government of the countryside, then and only then, could they make this 'green and pleasant land' the Jerusalem of their dreams.[22]

The metaphor Courtney uses of likening the AGM to a Parliament of Women or, as national newspapers were apt to call it, the 'Countrywoman's Parliament' is significant and ties in with the above quote. It implies both the exclusion of women from the Parliament at Westminster, but also the serious political nature of the meetings and their potential power. Yet Courtney like Robertson Scott before her, was keen to keep a sense of distance between the NFWI and the feminist movement. She describes in detail the movement's concern and involvement in issues like: the penalties of child assault, the legitimacy bill and its consequences, maternal mortality and the legal position of married women, as well as the rural women's position on issues which affected women less directly. Yet she says 'And they took no narrow feminist view'.[23] Then, as now, feminism was identified as a narrow, marginal, political line and thus invalid. Indeed, Courtney's notion of the NFWI, and any mass movement, is one which does not hold any ideas which may lead to conflict. Thus she advocates democracy or people power, providing the people come up with requests which will re-adjust the prevailing system without really threatening the power structures. Arguably such mass movements would make power structures more secure. So for example she claims:

> There is no trace as yet of the sort of evils that have beset so many other movements. There is no 'swerve to the left' or any other attempt on behalf of extremists to exert themselves ... If they are true to their principles, they should never engender class-warfare. Is there any risk of their engendering sex-warfare?[24]

Courtney seems to have a perception of combination in the form of trade unions or the Women's Institute Movement as being political, critical of the status quo and the conditions of oppression and as such acceptable. However, if they step beyond these areas and criticise the power structures and divisions within society which are arguably responsible for the rural deprivation she herself describes, then they become unacceptable. The boundaries she draws around acceptable and unacceptable political activity are the essence of British parliamentary democracy. She reiterates a common sense notion that participation in political debate and discussion is included within the definitions of Englishness, providing the essentially capitalist and male dominated nature of the nation is not criticised. Those who are active in popularly held definitions of feminism or left-wing politics are definitely excluded from the nation.

I am not trying to argue that the NFWI's identification with Englishness was negative. It was limiting, certainly, but it was also empowering. Identification of the WI members' interests as synonymous with those of the nation was able to be used as an important power base for improving the material conditions of rural women's lives. Nor would I want to argue that Courtney's version of the nation has nothing to offer the left or wasn't an important space won by women and the working class. It is one that should indeed be seen as significant in a period of history when the unions are able to be described as the 'enemy within' and rarely included in definitions of the nation. Rather, I would want to emphasise that the tension between empowerment and limitation, or incorporation and challenge, always existed. Finally she sums up her own perception of the NFWI, a definition by which they can be assimilated into perceptions of the nation and by which they can be included as 'people like us':

But the movement set one single aim before itself, the awakening and organising of the countrywomen into a force which should re-vitalise and raise to a higher level the life of the countryside. From its straight path to that goal it has turned neither to right nor to left.[25]

Perhaps this is also an indication of the seeds, even in the 1930s, that existed for the predominance of the political centre and the post-war consensus to follow in later years.

In 1943 Cicely McCall wrote a brief history of the NFWI and description of its activities for a series entitled *Britain in Pictures*.[26] The book, entitled simply *Women's Institutes*, must be seen as a product of the difficulties that an organisation like the NFWI was undergoing during the war. The NFWI refused to partake in activities which directly contributed to the preparation for war or the maintenance of hostilities during the war on the basis this would be against the principles of their Quaker members and thus exclude them from membership. (This is discussed more fully in chapter six). This laid them open to criticism from both inside and outside the organisation and like some other women's organisations their membership dropped, possibly to the benefit of the newly established Women's Royal Voluntary Service (WRVS). Cicely McCall was, at the time of writing the book, a full-time member of the NFWI staff, a post she resigned in 1945 to stand unsuccessfully as a Labour candidate in the General Election. Her history records the benefits to rural women of the WIs, saying for example: 'They had become part of country life and often the only bright part in the lives of thousands of countrywomen'.[27] She describes visits to the Albert Hall for the AGM, drama, handicrafts and other activities in the villages. Far more significantly, she describes the growing political consciousness and confidence developed through the NFWI by rural women. Issues were varied local campaigns such as to persuade a new local doctor to reinstate a surgery in the village or to build a village hall. However, McCall sees their significance, 'here was not only the perfect example of democracy at work but of training in citizenship'.[28] Attention is also drawn to national campaigns for women police and rural telephone boxes, for example. The NFWI's wartime work, jam and canning, and presenting the problems of evacuation from the rural women's point of view are also included in this history.

The emphasis of the book and of the more radical and feminist elements in the Movement are summed up in the last chapter entitled 'The Future':

Institutes have taught countrywomen to articulate, they have taught citizenship and revived forgotten crafts. As one member said, 'The Institute, it does broaden you.' Its self government has taught practical democracy, its classes and lectures have given members an opportunity to look beyond their village and beyond English shores.[29]

McCall pays little attention to drawing boundaries and there is no mention of the problems of feminism or left wing politics; instead, she is trying to change the definition of the nation from within. Her perception of the nation is able to include a more radically political notion of the NFWI, and by implication women, than previously expressed. Women are included and are central to the nation, the rural women in particular. They have, so to speak, earned their right to inclusion, to citizenship; in this the attention she gives to the WIs efforts on the Home Front, jam and canning centres, for example, are important. Obviously the historical specificity of this account is very significant. In a period of total war, all within the country who support the war are ideologically constructed as included within the nation. The excluded are obviously the enemy, the Germans, Fascists, Hitler, the Nazis – according to the construction. Left-wing groups such as the Communist Party (following the abandonment of the Hitler-Stalin pact) are involved in the war effort, as are women; they, at least briefly, are perceived as included. McCall perceives a significant future for the NFWI in post-war villages. She addresses the issues of ruralism, tradition and heritage. However, inclusion within and identification with the nation in these forms are used as part of what becomes a radical discourse to support demands for social welfare legislation:

> We shall want the wider experience and different outlook of younger members as well as the mature wisdom of older women if peace time villages are to be living units, not crumbling relics. Democracy has been well taught and practised in institutes, and when peace comes there will be 300,000 women ready to say loudly and clearly that since country people are 'custodians of a heritage' that heritage must be living, not embalmed. It must be drained and electrified, equipped with modern school buildings and an adequate school staff; it must have up-to-date health services and recreational facilities; and working women must be given a fair chance to take their part in planning and building the village life of the future.[30]

Thus from a point of inclusion, the NFWI and many other groups of feminists and those with left wing politics are able to challenge definitions of the nation and heritage and harness them to demand social welfare legislation. Thus ideas such as those in the Beveridge Report are able to be taken on board by the NFWI as the chapter on the 1940s will demonstrate.

In 1953 Inez Jenkins's official *History of the Women's Institute Movement* was published. This was very different from any previous history. It was above all an organisational history full of facts and figures, membership numbers and the development of the organisational structure. The book also focuses on the development of the subcommittees or main interest areas of the NFWI as perceived at the time; Produce, Farm and Garden, Kitchen and Market Stall and International Relations, for example, but in terms once again of the organisations such as the Produce Guild and the Associated Countrywomen of the World. Only in the last chapter 'A Little Light Relief', is there any space for the myths and stories of human experience so integral to the Robertson Scott history. For example, there is the story of the early VCO who at her inaugural talk in a village where she goes to start a WI finds herself confronted by a hall of men. At the end of the evening the men give her permission to come back and speak to their wives the following month. However, it is no longer a story demonstrating the need for women-only organisations to offer women an alternative culture, with all the possibilities for women to gain in confidence and assertiveness. Instead the story becomes a quaint and humorous aside. Within this history it is the organisation which is significant; the removal of stories such as this to a special chapter at the end entitled 'a little light relief' has marginalised them. Although folkstories and myths within an organisation may remain the same their meaning may be challenged, changed over time and different histories will contextualise such stories or myths. The reference to Mrs Watt knitting at the AOS meeting in the Jenkins's history loses much of its political significance and becomes once again quaint and anachronistic. The political bite has also been lost from Inez Jenkins's version of the Women's Institute Movement and may be seen as a thing of the past in this 'Whig' version of history. Women-centred local politics has apparently been superseded – presumably by the provision of water, sewage and electricity. For example, in the chapter 'Today and Tomorrow' she says:

It is in these different and differing villages that the institute movement must find its place. If in the modern village there is less need than of old for the institute as a spearhead of activity, the need remains, pronounced as ever, for what it can provide as a meeting place where skill and knowledge may be exchanged in friendliness, where there may be discussion without bias, where differences may be reconciled, where conflicting points of view may be understood and respected where the satisfaction and happiness of co-operative effort may be discovered and enjoyed.[31]

The definition of the community provided by and focused on the WI has become predominantly social, an exchange of domestic skills well organised and structured. The shift to a more inward-looking domestic NFWI may be seen to be in line with the higher profile that the media presented in the 1950s of the domestic role for women and notions of separate spheres.

Within the history there is little emphasis on the potentially feminist role of the movement and links with feminist organisations are played down or hardly mentioned. Indeed, the movement is portrayed as significantly owing its existence and style to a number of men and male organisations, for example, Mr Nugent Harris and Colonel Stapleton of the Agricultural Organisation Society. In the chapter on Farm Garden, Kitchen and Market stall, there is an example of this, 'After what we have learned of the beginning of the institute movement in this country and in Canada, it does not seem unnatural that the initiator of this activity was a man'.[32] This refers to the introduction of fruit canning to the movement. It could be an observation that female cultural space is only ever that allowed them by the dominant male culture. I think it is more than that; it is a negation of any conflict of interests or the power relationship between men and women. The dedication of the Jenkins's history also is worth examination:

> To those thousands of members whose names find no place in these pages yet who, by their shrewd sense of enterprise, their hard work, their courage, their rarely failing cheerfulness, their generosity in sharing skill and knowledge have enriched the life of their families, their villages, and their nation and make the Women's Institute Movement as we know it today in admiration and affection this book is dedicated.[33]

This then is her definition of those included in the movement and their perception of the nation. It gives precious little evidence of challenging the terms of inclusion. On the surface this seems to have taken several steps back from the 1930s and 1940s. Women and the NFWI appear to have accepted far more restrictive conditions for acceptance and inclusion within the nation. And yet although their struggle may have been less overt and less political, as I shall argue later in the final chapter, this may have been because they concentrated on local and immediate improvements in their material conditions within a separate female sphere.

Thus, it can be argued that the histories of the NFWI are about creating a sense of identity for the membership, a sense of belonging to a community and a tradition, although the defining nature of this community and tradition were constantly changing; being re-negotiated through them. They were also about placing the NFWI within a wider context to give the movement and its members a wider sense of belonging; fundamental to this was a sense of identification and inclusion within the nation. This necessitated the movement's other major identification; within the women's movement was somewhat precariously achieved. It was therefore the 'acceptable face of feminism', never directly referring to itself as feminist and always trying to distance itself from the more overt feminist movement. However, I do not want to put forward the NFWI's identification with the nation as something conspiratorial or even really conscious. I am almost sure it was not; at least not after the first few years when they had selected their motto 'For Home and Country'.

It is important always to be aware that such divisions and identifications around concepts such as the nation or the women's movement are principally ideological constructs, although they must at some level reinforce power blocs encouraging their perpetuation. Certainly, for the NFWI its identification and inclusion within the nation, within a notion of Englishness, was important in political terms and as a power base. The nation is not a static concept as I have tried to show, and as Cecily McCall's history shows it can be re-negotiated to serve left-wing and feminist causes. Any popular political movement has to engage in the struggle over the boundaries of the nation. However, it is also important, I feel, as a feminist historian to deconstruct such ideological boundaries because they obscure the continuity between different parts of the feminist movement. Consequently, they may hinder the potentially empowering perception of feminism as a plurality of voices, one of which was the Women's Institute Movement. Now after some sense of the changing perceptions of the Women's Institute Movement since its formation, it is necessary to return to the main concerns of the movement in the inter-war period.

NOTES

1. Stuart Hall, speaking at conference on the Nation and National Consciousness at Southampton University, June 1989.
2. P. Thane and J. Mackay, 'The Englishwoman', in P.Dodd and R.Colls (eds.), *Englishness, Politics and Culture*, Croom Helm, London 1986, p191.
3. *ibid.*
4. J.W. Robertson Scott, *The Story of the Women's Institute Movement in England and Wales*, Village Press, Idbury 1925.
5. *ibid.* pxi.
6. *ibid.* pvi.
7. *ibid.* p40.
8. *ibid.* p178.
9. *ibid.* p137.
10. *ibid.* pxii.
11. *ibid.* p148.
12. *ibid.* p148.
13. *ibid.* p1.
14. *ibid.* p33.
14. *ibid.* p15.
16. *ibid.* p22.
17. J.E. Courtney, *Countrywomen in Council*, London 1937.
18. J.E. Courtney, *The Adventurous Thirties – a Chapter in the Women's Movement*, Oxford University Press, Oxford 1933.
19. J.E. Courtney, *Countrywomen in Council*, London 1937, pi.
20. *ibid.* pvi.
21. *ibid.* p2.
22. *ibid.* p144.
23. *ibid.* p149.
24. *ibid.* p150.
25. *ibid.* p151.
26. Cicely McCall, *Women's Institutes*, London 1943.
27. *ibid.* p12.
28. *ibid.* p15.
29. *ibid.* p48.
30. *ibid.* p48.
31. Inez Jenkins, *The History of the Women's Institute Movement in England and Wales*, Oxford University Press, Oxford 1953, p151.
32. *ibid.* p105.
33. *ibid.* cover page.

4

POLITICS AND PATCHWORK

In order to be a truly popular organisation the NFWI needed to appeal across class, regional and age boundaries. This required it to have the capacity for its membership to create from it their own meanings according to their own particular circumstances and their position within the organisation. A middle-class spinster of independent means on a Southern County's executive would make sense of the movement in quite a different way from a working class mother of three in a Welsh village, or an aristocratic member of the National Executive. So far I have concentrated on looking at the histories of the NFWI, at its formation and on the meanings and interpretations of the leadership of the movement. In so doing, although indicating these changed, I have perhaps underplayed the contestation and conflict within the organisation. In this chapter I am going to concentrate on three areas which were central to the NFWI in the inter-war period and were the site of struggle. They are: the meaning of the organisation and its democratic structure, the development of arts and crafts work within the movement and, finally, attitudes towards domestic work and skill.

I intend to argue that there were widely different interpretations of what the organisation was about and how it should operate. These different interpretations were based not only on class, region and age but also on political viewpoints within the membership whereby Labour supporters were able to see the movement in terms of a Morris-style socialism; Liberals as an extension of the NUWSS style of feminism and Tories as an extension of their perception of English rural paternalism. This is not in any way to trivialise any of the viewpoints but to point out the NFWI's feminist potential. The Women's Institute Movement's feminism lies in the capacity such a large and diffuse organisation has for women to create their own meanings, their struggles to use it to re-negotiate the boundaries of femininity. A narrowly ideological definition of which struggles were feminist would inevitably have excluded or marginalised some women.

The right to work demanded by middle-class women in the 1920s and 1930s was not a feminist battle for the working-class women for whom the right to undertake one job, even if it was domestic labour, may have seemed preferable to undertaking two. If middle-class women's feminism was about the right to work, working-class women's struggle may often have been about the right to leisure. The debates within the movement over craft work and domesticity may exemplify these differences and contradictions; working-class women saw the movement predominantly in terms of a leisure provision, whereas many middle-class members saw it, at times, as providing them with something akin to an educationalist or social worker's work role, although it must be borne in mind that such class divisions are often somewhat blurred.

The Women's Institute Movement was a very wide and diffuse federal organisation and there was great variation in different institute activities and pre-occupations according to personnel. Chipping Camden, formed by a local peace group, was obviously going to be fairly involved in peace campaigns. Alternatively, Henfield in West Sussex, which had former actress and then suffrage campaign writer Elizabeth Robins as its President and numbered writer Margaret Macnamara amongst its members, had a strong drama group and the Fabian Maud Pember Reeves to speak at one of its meetings. (See Appendix One as an example of a WI annual programme). Consequently, the typicality of meanings, interpretations and conflicts that I offer here are open to question. Despite this I hope they will demonstrate the feminist potential of the organisation and give an alternative impression of the movement in the inter-war years to that offered by the official histories. First, it is necessary to address the organisation itself within the villages.

Local WIs were run by a committee elected by secret ballot. Letters to *Home and Country* indicate the democratic system did not quite run as smoothly as it might and certainly its ideas were quite alien to rural England where the voting for parish councillors was still not by secret ballot. The President of Singleton, in the 1920s, wrote to headquarters to confirm her view that any canvassing was unacceptable – presumably because it might challenge her inalienable right to re-election. She was to be disappointed with the reply. Another letter wonders whether a ruling could not be introduced to prevent more than one member of any family being on the committee. In her village six committee members came from three families, implying a sort of village mafia, despite there being over thirty nominations. Membership of the committee was not always considered desirable. In some areas a lack of willingness by the gentry or the middle classes to be on the committee was considered shirking their duty. A diary kept between 1918 and 1923 by Mrs Huddart, a VCO in Sussex, relayed in December 1921 the traumas suffered by a WI when the gentry were unwilling to play their role:

> A difficulty arose about a President. None wished to take the post, at last Mrs Isaac Knight consented but no one would be Vice President, Secretary or Treasurer. It was suggested that it should be put to the meeting whether the WI should continue.[1]

This resolution was not put; instead the issue was postponed until the next month when it was decided to continue for another six months. By the time of this meeting various women had been press-ganged into being officers and Mrs Huddart remarked 'The members appeared to enjoy the meeting ... The members seem to be very anxious to keep the institute going'.[2] In Coopers Cross Institute there is an indication that the ordinary working-class members of the institute were able to use the WI for their own ends, but the problem lay in the unwillingness of the social elite to fulfil their expected role. Certainly, in most institutes the middle classes tended to be well represented on WI committees. The vicar's wife was unlikely to escape without holding some sort of office, frequently as treasurer or secretary, although in oral interviews some have expressed something less than total enthusiasm for this arrangement. In an account of Scarcliffe WI given by Mrs Green, she found herself as a young teacher the secretary of the WI started by the headmaster's wife. She seems to have had a fairly hard time of it, remembering 'We didn't have subcommittees for various jobs. I seemed to do everything; arrange for speakers, tea hostesses, competitions, roll-call even accommodation for some of the speakers'.[3]

The potential headaches involved in the election of the first committee at a new local Institute is described in a *Home and Country* article, written in the first person entitled 'Our Valiant VCOs':

> The chairwoman is full of agitation which she does her best to communicate to the VCO.
>
> We can't have Mrs Henn and Miss Pullett on the committee together. It is well known that as fast as one walks into the room the other walks out.

We must elect Mrs Wyandotte. She'll be so hurt if we don't. Shall I just go round and tell them all that they must vote for Mrs Wyandotte?

Lady Rock will have to be President of course. Its rather a pity that she spends half the year abroad and in London the rest of the time, but of course she's the one to be President.

I deal as tactfully as may be with the chairman's suggestions make another speech all about the necessity of having a representative committee and collect the ballot papers. When the names of the committee are read aloud, there is more applause but I am again approached by the chairwoman.

We can't have Mrs Barnshaw of the butcher's shop on the committee. Quite impossible. You must take her off again.

Why?

She's a Bolshevik, says the chairwoman, whose political sympathies obviously lie in the opposite direction.

But the movement is essentially non-party political. She won't talk Bolshevism at your monthly meetings, because that would be against the rules.

She doesn't hold with the King, says the chairwoman in a thrilling whisper.

I am sorry to hear this, but explain that I can do nothing about it and that Mrs Barnshaw having been duly elected must be welcomed by the rest of the committee as cordially as if her views were more orthodox.

It is a relief, after we have had tea and congratulated one another on having got the Institute started, to notice that Mrs Barnshaw joins as lustily at singing the national anthem as we bring the meeting to a close.[4]

This extract demonstrates a variety of things; its message is one of determination to keep to the principle of election and democracy, even if the reality is not quite so straightforward. It is interesting to note that an attempt to debar absentee committee and office holders failed to gain support at a 1928 Consultative Council meeting. Many institutes presumably were aware that within a village, patronage and the role of the gentry on a committee was not necessarily assessed in terms of the practical work they did. Significantly, the notion that all political persuasions have a place in the WI is held along with the reassurance that the allegations about Mrs Barnshaw from the butcher's as a representative political extremist were basically only rumours.

Elections also took place from the institutes for County and

National Executives, although co-opting occurred to the National Executive which often then led to members selection by ballot the next year. Policy decisions were made at the National AGM although a selection process about which resolutions to vote on occurred before this. It has to be pointed out that those involved in National and County level organisation, as well as those attending AGMs and Consultative Councils, were rarely working class. As well as the operation of class hegemony, there were practical reasons for this. It was, for example, a problem for working-class women to get away from their homes and domestic responsibilities. A Shropshire member who described herself as a working-class onlooker and who praised Shropshire for having a working-class Vice-Chairman on the County Executive said in 1924, 'the only reason that more working women are not on this particular county committee is a question of time required to attend meetings. This is chiefly due to the train service'.[5] In Scarcliffe WI attendance at county meetings was decided not by ballot but once again by practicalities – 'As delegates we went to Derby by train – steam not diesel! My landlady's husband was a railway worker and as she had concessionary tickets she usually went to these meetings'.[6]

With the exception of one year when it moved to Blackpool, the AGM was held in London at the Royal Albert Hall and delegates tended to be committee members or middle-class and middle-aged, but not necessarily. *The Daily News* relayed the following story:

> A woman representing a Hampshire village was afraid of venturing alone to London and brought a fellow member with her. They presented themselves at the door of the hall hand in hand and since each institute may be represented by only one delegate, it was suggested one of them should visit the picture house over the way while the other attended the conference. The suggestion that they should both part so scared them, however, that at length a concession was made and they were both admitted.[7]

For those two women at least the AGM had provided a unique and if at first intimidating experience, certainly one which would challenge their perceptions of themselves as rural housewives, whereas a delegate from Churchingford in Somerset who wrote in *Home and Country* of her day at the AGM in 1939, described a jam-packed twenty-nine hours most of which consisted of sightseeing. With another delegate she had walked all round London to look at the Royal Palaces and other places of architectural interest before breakfast, been to an ice rink and even a film in the early evening. Her only reference to the meeting was to remark 'I won't say anything about the meeting except – why must we have a man to play the organ for us?'.[8] This remark underlines the importance, to the women involved, of the women-only nature of the organisation and the achievement of the meeting in which even a male on the organ is seen as an invasion of hard fought for female space. Holding the AGM in Blackpool in 1930 resulted in one institute sending its youngest member on the basis that she really should see Blackpool. How Blackpool was decided upon and why it was never repeated, other than cost, I am not clear. There is always a sort of tension between the serious and the frivolous in any such events and it certainly seemed to err too closely on the side of leisure rather than business. A poem published in *Home and Country* about an aunt who went to the Blackpool conference armed with notes and directives from her Institute, only to be lured away by the pleasure beach and never seen again, is an indication of concern about whether Blackpool was suitable for the AGM.[9]

The institutes in the villages operated around a monthly meeting backed up by classes as varied as folkdancing or dressmaking, a number of fundraising social events, such as whist drives or village socials and a yearly outing. The meeting consisted of: the business (a term used to refer to any local or national organisational matters), one or two talks or demonstrations, tea (known as 'the cement' of the movement) and the entertainment half-hour. A variety of games, dancing, singing or acting would make up this entertainment; a great success in Trent WI was a grandmothers' race. Each grandmother, provided with a glass of milk, spoon and bib, raced to a grown-up baby and fed it; the first to return received a prize. Getting the regular membership to attend the talks in both mind and body often proved a little difficult. If, as I mentioned earlier, Funtington in West Sussex could get one hundred and fifty people to a dance it could only muster thirty for a talk on 'making something out of nothing'. It was not alone in this problem as minute books show. Furthermore the discerning membership, according to records, show a definite inclination to chat, knit or snooze through any subject they felt uninteresting or irrelevant. The topics were wide-ranging, although the minutes of Appuldram in Chichester[10] in the 1920s record that the committee did not feel that a proposed talk on VD and public hygiene was necessary.

If there were problems with ordinary meetings, then any suggestions from county or national officers could fare even worse. *Home and Country* frequently ran articles which indicate the awareness of the leadership with different attitudes to local institute events. One is entitled 'The Roll Call'. A vicar's wife who is president of a small institute is encouraged by a local VCO to have a roll call. It is explained thus: 'the idea is to make all the members talk and be friendly together so we ask them the same question and they answer it in turns'. The choice of question 'What improvement would you most like in your house?' also indicates a wish to raise the membership's consciousness and precipitate discussion over a key WI concern, raising the standard of rural housing. The first four members refuse to say anything without more warning and the next four all opt for electricity and the next two for a wireless. One woman feels her house would be best knocked down altogether, which is not well received by her landlady sitting nearby. As the next two women opt for a lodger and a husband respectively the president decides to unanimous approval that it must be tea-time.[11] For these women the importance of the event lay in the fun and camaraderie of other women rather than in discussing social reforms whose implementation seemed remote and unlikely. It was not just the membership for whom the female companionship and an alternative female culture is important. E.M. Delafield was a VCO and writer who fictionalised her experiences in a regular column for the feminist magazine *Time and Tide* under the title of *Diary of a Provincial Lady*. She found herself in a number of situations; judging darning competitions for which she felt singularly unqualified due to her own incompetence in that direction and constantly having her whole household hunt for her NFWI membership badge as she left to speak at a local WI. She undertook a three day speaking tour of local institutes which involved her on one night freezing in a manor house with a geriatric deaf member of the aristocracy for company. However, her description of her next night is one of women's culture which will not be unfamiliar to women today:

> We talk about the movement's annual meeting at Blackpool, perhaps a mistake, why not Bristol or Plymouth? difficulty of thinking up new programmes for monthly meetings, and really magnificent performance of Chick at recent folk dancing rally at which institute members called upon to go through 'Gathering Peascods' no less than three times – two of Chicks best performers says assistant secretary being grandmothers. I

express astonished admiration, and we go on to village halls, Sir Oswald Mosley, and methods of removing ink-stains from linen. Just as Assistant Secretary, who is unmarried and lives in a nice little cottage – has escorted me to charming little bedroom, she remembers I am eventually going to Crimpington, and embarks on interesting scandal about two members of Institute there and unaccountable disappearance of one members name from the committee. This keeps us up till eleven o'clock when she begs me to say nothing whatever about her having mentioned the affair, which was all told her in the strictest confidence.[12]

Indeed, for many women it may have been belonging to an all-women group which was most important. A place where, instead of being 'the Other', women were central and could explore issues, learn new skills, challenge their own internalisation of a socially constructed subservience whilst raising both their confidence and their consciousness. The regular meeting of a large group of women in a village in the 1920s or 1930s in itself would necessitate a change of perceptions about male and female spheres. This would be magnified when the women took over the local pub – as they did in Singleton, West Sussex, once a month, a fairly significant appropriation of male space. In other areas the WI were instrumental in building a WI or a village hall which became a female-controlled social centre for the village, an alternative to the male dominated space of the pub. A village hall built by the WI was able to become a physical manifestation of women's power and ability.

Local institutes also ran a series of social events for the whole village. The WI social held at Christmas-time (and sometimes at other times of the year) was very popular. It included entertainment by WI members, supper and dancing and yet there is every indication that the men who attended these events – only if accompanying WI members – found them uncomfortable, as numerous humorous articles written in *Home and Country* indicate. They found the gender relations implied in women-controlled events difficult to handle. Within the WI social men were marginalised, they became outsiders, visitors within a female-defined culture and value system. An article entitled 'That Social' in 1929 *Home and Country* written from a male point of view and in their own particular form of rural dialect begins:

'You could have gone an knocked me down with a feather', said Ephram Pepperwot.

'When my ole Susan asked me to go to that there Women's Institute Social'.

'Thought you didn't allow husbands and such like heathen', I says.

'Not at our ordinary meeting we don't', says she. 'Still to the social husbands can come if accompanied by a member'.

'Not admitted except on a leash' I says sarcastic.

'If you take it that way', says she.

The article goes on to describe the supper and the dancing:

'It was a new kind of dancing called folkdancing which isn't rightly new, but a very old kind, same as they used to dance in the days when they used to call this country Merrie England which must have been a long time ago.'[13]

This article indicates to me that the female readership knew of the male discomfort and positively revelled in their sense of 'Otherness'. Thus the meaning of the movement was varied. It could provide a significant female controlled cultural space for women who had, in rural areas previously, had few such opportunities. The democratic structure was in reality regarded by the members often with a very large pinch of salt. AGMs might be regarded as a social jaunt and the village élite expected to put in the donkey work to organise institute activities which the working-class membership would utilise in a way that made sense in their lives; however, one area where this led to conflict was in the growing involvement by the movement, in the 1920s and 1930s, in craftwork to which I now want to turn.

There were in the early 1920s a series of different strands and contradictions to the NFWI craftwork. The first involved the commercial production of craftwork and helping principally working-class members to engage in some form of non-exploitative homework. Alternatively, there was the amateur, but highly skilled work engaged in by the mainly middle-class women focused around the Guild of Learners. Although this work was amateur it fitted at some level into middle-class women's need for an outlet for their creative energies which can be aligned with a culture of work. Thus they looked for work satisfaction, a skilled status, a structured system of achievement and advancement. There was some conflict and contestation around definitions of suitable crafts between the different strands though the boundaries and divisions were always clearly defined; some middle-class women found the crafts an acceptable way of earning money as women in the Arts and Crafts Movement had previously.[14] It is also necessary to bear in mind constructions and divisions around gender and definitions of craft and art. Craft has predominantly been that engaged in by women and the working class while definitions of art have been controlled primarily by groups within the white male bourgeoisie. The boundaries of art and craft as suitable male and female spheres were, however, being contested before the formation of Women's Institutes by the Arts and Crafts movement with whom the Women's Institute Movement had significant connections. May Morris was secretary of her local WI and W.R. Lethaby (who had strong connections with William Morris) was a very frequent contributor to *Home and Country*, challenging and deconstructing boundaries between art and craft, between male and female spheres. This cannot be done merely by redefining an individual craft in terms of art or making it acceptable for women to do, as this leaves the very structure of such divisions untouched, much as women's steady shift into clerical work at the end of the nineteenth century, or for that matter the 'new man's' take-over of cooking, has left the divisions between male and female work, in and out of the home, untouched. What is necessary is to deconstruct the very boundaries of art and craft, which are also tied up with ideas of public and private consumption, utilitarian and decorative, commercial and leisure production. NFWI craftwork become an area for the contestation of many of these boundaries and divides.

A wide variety of craft-style local industries developed within the movement with a suitable number of different commercial outlets to match them. National organisation of commercial craftwork was unsuccessful because of the huge difficulties in maintaining any uniformity of standard and consistency of supply throughout an organisation as diffuse as the NFWI. This was a significant factor in the financial failure of the WI Toy Society which had a short life from 1918–1919. The Toy Society, in which local institutes who wanted to participate had to purchase a share, supplied instructors and materials and handled sales. The response from the institutes was far greater than expected and not enough instruction and management was able to be provided to the WIs involved. It was under-capitalised for the number of potential participants, not on a very commercial footing and suffered from competition from abroad and uneven standards. It closed down in April 1919 with Lady Denman out of pocket, but not greatly so. Localised, specialised industries capitalising on local skills and materials and small enough for the degree of control necessary for a consistent standard to be maintained were found to be more successful. Ticehurst smocks, which developed out of a smocking class, sold to major London stores such as Liberty's up until World War Two. *Home and Country* in 1920 listed a variety of industries WIs were engaged in: artificial flower-making, fur gloves from rabbit skins, Buckinghamshire pillow lace, dolls and toy animals, rush basket-making and chair-caning. One of the most successful was Micheldever WI in Hampshire with rush- and sedge-making. This industry, which had a local tradition, was started with the aim of entering the first WI exhibition at Caxton Hall in 1917. Initial instruction came from a man in a neighbouring village who could remember the previously dying craft. They received not only the prizes for their section, but for the best example of any industry exhibited at Caxton Hall. By 1922 the women were making mats, baskets, rush bottoms for chairs, log baskets, hats, kneelers, table mats and carrying out orders for places as far afield as Scotland, Africa and New Zealand. The women were involved in the whole process of: cutting, drying, plaiting and making up the articles.[15] Some local institutes like Ticehurst and Micheldever organised particular crafts, but it was more common for the WI to act as a training ground and then sales point for individuals or pairs of craftswomen. This was done at a variety of different points, every institute meeting had a sales table, but more significant were WI trading depots and the highly successful Women's Institute markets.

Hampshire Women's Institutes, as a Federation, had a strong commitment to industries and in April 1919 a county teacher of crafts was appointed to help teach institutes, as low standards and shoddy workmanship were thought acute problems. A series of fundraising efforts were held in 1920 with the aim of setting up craftwork premises. Samples of the industry's work had to be sent before a judging committee with the express intention of keeping up the standard of work. It also gave county organisers a fair perception of standards of work and specialisation in various institutes. This was to stand them in good stead when they obtained orders from four London department stores for toys. The depot trading centre opened in Winchester in October 1920, well-timed for the Christmas season. Indeed the centre was at first so successful that a full-time manager was appointed in early December as the volume of work was too great for voluntary helpers. The depot also linked with two disabled men's wooden toy industries. Maidstone in Kent also had a depot from 1919 which began as a centre principally for selling jam – a particularly successful cottage industry in Kent WIs. The centre also had a rest room and club premises. In its heyday it was not only selling jam, but acting as a point of sale for institutes selling towels to the baby clinics and someone else ordering a wedding trousseau. However, its success was short-lived, like most of the WI depots, and in 1922 it was severely depressed, closing in 1926 apparently due to political difficulties. The depots operated as a model in many ways for the WI markets which followed. WI markets ranged then as now, from being open one day a week, to every day, and sold on commission. They did not restrict themselves to WI members and often sold work produced by small-holders, the disabled and ex-servicemen. Membership required buying at least one share; as they were a co-operative venture there was a limit on the number of shares it was possible to purchase. They sold much more, however, in the way of food and agricultural produce than craftwork. For the women who sold successfully through such parts of the NFWI there was the chance to earn much needed cash in a rather less exploitive way than most homework offered. Economic power provided for women through work is often important and for rural women for whom work was severely contracting this was significant. Furthermore, within a capitalist economy validation comes through the marketplace. Thus the importance for many women in any form of paid work is not merely in terms of what the money can buy, it is also in placing value on their activities which, however necessary they may be, capitalism does not value.

As the history of Micheldever rush and sedge industry demonstrated, national and local exhibitions were a vital part of the development of handicrafts, particularly from the point of selling and developing markets. Also exhibitions place crafts which have previously operated within the private domain into the sphere of the public. Pen Dalton argued in *Women and Craft* that there are a variety of reasons why it is positive for their craftwork to be exhibited:

> It provides evidence of women's culture and history.
>
> It challenges the notions of great art.
>
> It brings the values associated with it to the forefront. Values like caring, modesty and gentleness which have been socially associated with femininity and therefore devalued.

She concludes:

> Communicating through craft can give the woman tied to the home a voice outside to penetrate and influence the dominant sphere of cultural exchange. Unless we speak out and in any form available to us, we can never hope to gain access to the means of owning and controlling the institutions of power that circumscribe and determine our lives as housewives.[16]

This may be especially important in relation to craftwork not concerned with earning money directly but with saving money or materially improving the welfare of the family through women's efforts. A contributor to *Home and Country* stressed the significance of this side of craftwork saying, 'In a time of economic stress such as the present, craftwork in the Women's Institutes has an opportunity to prove its usefulness and to give material help in the home life of the nation'.[17] Arguably when the construction of rag rugs, children's clothes etc. leads to displays in exhibitions or winning awards for such items, the labour within them is recognised and this recognition remains after the item has been used and perished. This may be very validating for women, so much of whose domestic labour is about the return to the status quo; houses are cleaned, family and children fed, but all will start again tomorrow. Prizes in competitions and exhibitions; a fixed value placed on domestic labour by some goods being sold through the WI, recognises and records female domestic labour as the wage packet does for the man. Furthermore, the exhibition celebrates the skill of such female domestic labour and challenges its place within both women and men's value systems. However, the market place has a contaminating influence from the point of view of art. For a product to be considered art within our culture it cannot be financially viable; indeed, catering to the market place may be seen as vulgarisation. Sales can validate a product which élite groups who definine art or even craft, may find unacceptable; within the NFWI crinoline ladies, papier mâché goods, gollywogs all fell into this category of unacceptable craftwork. The notion that craftsmanship and saleability are in conflict arises again when in *Home and Country* the NFWI handicrafts advisor argues, 'For a worker to make things that to her are ugly merely because they will sell, shows that the true spirit of craftsmanship is lacking'. It also shows that the spirit of industry and commercial viability is alive and kicking, always working on the assumption that the movement's membership has the same interpretation of ugly as the NFWI leadership, a point which is open to question.

L. Preece (the advisory director of handicrafts to the NFWI) wrote a series of articles and snippets in *Home and Country* under the title 'Notes on Handicrafts'. Her perception of craft is as something of practical use; but it also carries the connotations of nostalgia and heritage with which craft, in the wake of William Morris and the Arts and Crafts Movement was by then associated. There was not, however, a simplistic acceptance of this rarification of past methods and in *Home and Country* in March 1933 a heated debate went on as to whether the hand loom was redundant as the proper bought machine may produce the best results for those who refuse to constantly copy the past. Preece's column announced the formation of the Guild of Learners in 1920, which was to offer 'Special assistance ... for those Institute members who wish to use leisure time in the practice of home crafts'. Its aims were to be:

> 1] to regain the practice of Home Handicrafts with a view to restore the best traditions of English workmanship
> 2] To assist in bringing the best instruction in handicraft within the reach of the village.[18]

Membership was in two categories: associate membership for those undertaking to become proficient in some craft connected in the home, those already proficient and those prepared to teach handicrafts had full membership. The guild was to organise a variety of tests with two levels – for those who wanted to practise a craft and those who wanted to teach. The use of the word 'Guild' in the title was very significant, implying the skilled status with which this group identified themselves. By 1937 there were tests in thirty-seven crafts including plain sewing and embroidery. In practice this group became the standard setters for NFWI handicrafts. Those crafts which were tested by the Guild of Learners were significant, genuine; those that weren't were marginalised. (A sample year, 1922, of the Guild of Learners is in Appendix 2 at the end of the chapter.) The tensions over what were acceptable crafts became more fervent over time, with the NFWI handicrafts advisor, the NFWI handicrafts subcommittee and the Guild of Learners being the arbitrators of acceptability. Significant in their being able to do this is of course their control over the appointment of craft teachers and their hold over NFWI handicraft spending. In the 1920s the NFWI had been given a government grant to help with handicraft teaching. Alice Armes in 1930 states her position as handicraft advisor very clearly:

> The individual naturally is free either to make good use of, or waste her time as she pleases and if she wishes to fill her house from top to bottom with painted fish bones, sealing wax beads, paper flowers etc. no one can prevent her, but she can not expect that exhibitions can be made a dumping ground for such useless work or certificates for craftsmanship given to it.[19]

The idea that the craft should in some way be utilitarian is brought into play here but defintions of usefulness were, like so many other areas of NFWI craftwork, the subject of controversy. Many of the handicrafts demonstrated at monthly meetings in the villages were aimed at making women more self-sufficient, reminiscent of Cobbett's *Cottage Economy*.[20] In this category would come all sorts of practical skills – cobbling, chimney-sweeping, jam-making and clothes-making – enabling women to be more independent both from industrial capitalism and their husbands. For example, in 1921 Hutton WI had a demonstration on cobbling when the speaker according to the minutes 'heeled a shoe in fine style'. So enthusiastic were the members about this craft that the institute held classes and acquired a set of cobbling tools which members could borrow at 6d a day. Such action was of real financial benefit to the members.

There was a tension between the notion of practicality or the usefulness of craft articles and displays of skill, particularly in relation to exhibitions. M. Somerville, giving advice with regard to suitable items for the London exhibitions, argued that an exhibit should show as much craftsmanship as possible, compatible with good taste.[21] Who defined good taste and how was a matter of furious debate. Toys were failed on the Guild of Learners Toy Test for forgetting the child's point of view, but there was also a demand that those who did understand children should have the patience to master the technicalities. A differentiation was required between exhibition work and work of general utility. This was demonstrated to a handicraft expert at a County Show when a member pointed out 'You don't want a lot of stitching in children's things as its always in the wash-tub, but then of course you wouldn't be expected to know that. I've got six and

I know what washing day is'.[22] This distinction between work for utility in the home and for an exhibition displayed the very middle-class origins of most of the exhibitors. Working-class women could neither afford the materials nor the time to make items for exhibition only. A correspondent to *Home and Country* in the early 1930s pointed out that the working class can only justify craft if it is saleable, or presumably as a necessity for the household. What these arguments all indicate is that by this time the exhibitions were a specialised area. This seems to have caused no small degree of antagonism. There were demands for special classes for working women who had not the time or facilities for the more advanced work and whose hands, roughened by the manual labour of rural housewifely tasks, were not felt appropriate for finer needlecraft. There were demands for separate classes for the cottage and leisured classes – cottage being a euphemism for working class. One letter to *Home and Country* pointed out :

> I know of many members who will not exhibit for the simple reason that the their exhibits are judged on the same plane as those of the leisured classes and on the same plane as those who have been taught by the Guild of Learners school.[23]

By the early 1930s exhibits at the London Exhibition were almost totally from Guild of Learners members, often those who held an A certificate and were teachers. One of the few exhibition entries in which ordinary members could take part was co-operative quilt-making: where twenty or thirty members of one institute between them constructed a quilt, often patchwork. This co-operative venture, by the very number of those participating in its production, challenged perceptions of art and craft being the result of individual skill or talent and provided a focus for women to get together, chat, gossip and have some form of female-centred leisure. That it was done around quilt making may say more about women's uneasy relationship to leisure than crafts. A female culture and camaraderie was thus able to be developed within the quilting clubs, a member of a North Country WI quilting club recalled:

> We always used to meet about two o' clock and hope to work till four and then stop and have a cup of tea. And we used to make scones, and a sandwich cake or something and we would share it out. We used to enjoy it. All the tales that we told over the quilting frame. Well you

could imagine. Everything was discussed, it was really entertainment making quilts.[24]

Thus co-operative quilt-making had a role to play in allowing women to carve out some leisure time as well as challenging definitions of art and individual creativity. Although there were some isolated areas which managed, despite the difficulties of the 1930s, to maintain crafts upon a commercial setting, for the working class at least craft became predominately a leisure activity or for home consumption. The members showed a healthy disregard for the definitions of acceptable craft put forward by those in the NFWI Craft Movement leadership. Both oral interviews and local records relate women sticking shells or pictures on boxes and various other pursuits which did not fit into the leadership's definition of suitable crafts. For these women such activities represented a struggle to carve out space for leisure, to do their own thing, which was difficult without some utilitarian element. It was also a celebration of women's or housewives' diverse and inevitably acquired practical skills to produce something with a little more permanence than most housework. For some members it was also a way of exerting control over their environment through their own creativity. Despite, or perhaps because of, the different roles craft played in members' lives it remained a very significant part of the Women's Institute Movement.

Some common ground could be found across the divisions within the NFWI craft movement in the ideas of W.R. Lethaby which were perhaps influenced by William Morris's *News from Nowhere*.[25] Lethaby, who wrote frequently for *Home and Country* argued that even day-to-day tasks can be defined as art, or raised to the status of art. These notions, that even laying a table is an art, a skill, were used by NFWI members to support their perception of the housewife as a skilled worker. Thus the movement, from within their female value system, could challenge the dominant culture's perception of housework and domesticity. It is from such an alternative set of meanings that some of the movement's apparently traditional views on women's role should be seen. For example, in June 1928 Fernhurst WI in West Sussex had a debate on the subject 'Should husbands cook the Sunday dinner?' It was decided they should not, although 'wives would accept thankfully any help their husbands offered'.[26] At its most fundamental level this is women determinedly hanging on to one of the only power relationships they have, that of food production and at that point in the week where it is given most status and centrality as a family ritual. Their conclusion to the debate can also be seen as a reflection of women's perception of their role as a skilled one and therefore, like any other skilled person, they were not going to diminish their skill by letting themselves be replaced by an unskilled labourer, even once a week. Indeed, even handling husbands falls into the same category of a skill, exercised by the efficient housewife like any other skill, hence in 1922 at Worpledon WI a recipe is given to assist:

> Take of punctuality, cleanliness and cheerfulness as much as you can secure. Add a strong belief in good motives when anything offends, and let the ambition to make tart replies stand still until quite cool. Flavour strongly with unwavering love and truth and having grilled the tongue upon the fine patience, serve up with a smile without sauce. Ready forgiveness is the most graceful ornament and is sure to be much appreciated. NB If the weather is rather stormy, silence is a valuable addition and will be found a relish.[27]

Although tongue-in-cheek this could be read as an endorsement for traditional domesticity; however, within the WI context, I do not think it was. Rather it fits more with a female attitude to men so often found in discussions in toddler groups and at school gates, as somehow childlike, incapable of the most menial tasks and really on a par with children. Handling menfolk becomes another domestic chore along with washing and cleaning but, like them, one which is a skill.

Being acknowledged as a skilled worker as opposed to a housewife was tied up with the right to time off work, to leisure. This was an important element of the Women's Institute Movement. As well as the craftwork a whole variety of other areas developed: drama, folk singing and dancing, village socials, day trips and outings. These women-organised trips represented an appropriation of leisure previously unknown to rural women. Mrs Curly Brown of Somerset was heard to say 'I have always wanted to travel and now it is going to be possible through the WI'.[28] However ideologically constructed the places for outings may have been (there were a lot of trips to stately homes), how they were perceived and the meanings placed on them remained firmly within the power of the members. When that same Mrs Curly Brown visited Cheddar Gorge in the 1920s it was not the stalagmites which impressed her but the electric lighting.[29] Although many of the activities, like folkdancing and drama, were arranged around competitive events there was nothing like the contention over them that there was over craftwork. Participation was genuinely much more cross class and indeed, far more working-class women took part. Such events within a women's group were significant for confidence-raising and helped to challenge dominant perceptions of femininity. Women's ability to do things when men are not present, their discovery of a different atmosphere, confidence and relaxation tends to lead to a questioning of why it is and how it is that they are not normally able to behave in such ways in the presence of men.

As a large federal organisation with a membership across both class and age lines, the NFWI's ideology, its meaning to its membership, cannot easily be identified given the passage of time. What can unquestionably be contended is that it provided a female space within which women could create different value systems and meanings from the dominant ones in society.

The Women's Institute Movement was in the inter-war period a female cultural space, within which skills were learnt by women and confidence gained. It also provided a few women with the opportunity to engage in non-exploitable craftwork; many more found a space to engage in women-centred leisure. In the next chapter I want to turn to the more serious side of the NFWI; how they became involved in campaigns for improved rural housing and water supplies. It demonstrates how their new found confidence as skilled workers and their perception of themselves as the heart of the nation, were able to be transferred into demands for social welfare legislation. Rural housing and water are concerns that are central to the movement throughout the period covered by this history and so have been examined as a case study on their own; rather than within the more historically specific chapters.

NOTES

1. Mrs Huddart, unpublished diary kept in ESFWI archive, 15 December 1921.
2. *ibid.*, 25 January 1922.
3. Mrs Green, written personal history of her activities in the WI in History file in the NFWI archive.
4. *Home and Country*, January 1927, p16.
5. *Home and Country*, April 1924, p17.
6. Mrs Green, *op cit*.
7. *The Daily News*, 2 June 1927.
8. *Home and Country*, July 1939, p169.

9. *Home and Country*, July 1930, p346-7.
10. Appuldram WI minute books, 1927, in WSFWI archives.
11. *Home and Country*, May 1936, p231-3.
12. E.M. Dellafield, *Diary of a Provincial Lady*, London 1930, reprinted Virago, London 1984, p115.
13. *Home and Country*, January 1929, p32-3.
14. A. Callen, *Angel in the Studio*, Astragal, London 1979, gives a good account of women in the arts and crafts movement.
15. *Home and Country*, August 1922, p8-9.
16. P. Dalton, 'Housewives, Leisure Crafts, Ideology: De-skilling in Consumer Craft', in G. Elinor *et al* (eds.), *Women and Craft*, Virago, London 1987, p36.
17. *Home and Country*, July 1931, p212.
18. *Home and Country*, July 1920, p3.
19. *Home and Country*, February 1930, p93.
20. W. Cobbett, *Cottage Economy*, 1821, reprinted Kensington 1926.
21. *Home and Country*, April 1922, p6.
22. *ibid.*
23. *Home and Country*, August 1928, p380.
24. Quoted in P. Kirkham, 'The Inter-War Years Handicraft Revival', in J. Attfield (ed.), *A View from the Interior Feminism Women and Design*, Women's Press, London 1989, p179.
25. W. Morris, *News from Nowhere*, 1891, reprinted Routledge, London 1970.
26. Fernhurst WI Minute books, 1928, in WSFWI archives.
27. Worpledon WI records, 1922, in WSFWI archives.
28. 'Up-long-down-a-long members memoirs of WI outing' in History file in the NFWI archives.
29. *ibid.*

5

CAMPAIGNS

The Women's Institute Movement's motto was 'For Home and Country' and in their campaigns to improve rural housing, the elevation of the domestic sphere contained in this motto and pragmatic political action to improve the lot of rural women were entwined. Although decent housing remains a basic necessity for the healthy reproduction of the workforce, by whom and how it should be provided is controversial. Similarly, what constitutes good enough or adequate housing is open to debate on gender and class lines, with a huge gap culturally, as often as not, in terms of class and gender between those who design and control working-class housing and those who live in it. Within these debates, this contestation, the struggles over building a consensus around the definition of adequate housing, the NFWI and other pressure groups can play a significant role. In this chapter I shall look at how the movement contributed towards the building of just such a consensus. It is only one example of how the movement, at both a local and national level, was able to develop its own particular version of feminist politics in which the links between the personal and the political were always present. There were many more political and social welfare campaigns in which they were involved: women police, analgesics for rural women in childbirth, equal pay and equal compensation for war injuries, to name but a few.

Both water and housing were on the political agenda for the Women's Institute Movement throughout the first forty-five years of their history. They were constantly the focus of NFWI activity in terms of AGM and Consultative Council resolutions, NFWI surveys and articles in *Home and Country*. At a local level institutes had talks and undertook a variety of pressure group-style activities. For example, Warninglid WI in East Sussex had lectures on subjects related to the home in the 1920s and 1930s, which included beauty in the home, whereas *Home and Country* included instructions on the best way to maintain an earth closet and the AGM in the 1940s demanded the nationalisation of water and sewage.[1] Demands for more rural council houses and improved designs were frequent. The NFWI concern with housing was at basically three levels. Firstly, the ideological, that is, issues around re-negotiating the culturally held perceptions of the home and the domestic worker within it; secondly, the pragmatic, which included anything that housewives could do individually to improve the efficiency, atmosphere or physical environment of the home; and finally, political action to improve the material conditions of working-class homes. It should be borne in mind, however, that some NFWI demands, such as for builders to place water pipes inside or to lag them to prevent them freezing, were not applicable to working-class homes only. Within this chapter I shall look very briefly at the Women's Institute Movement's ideological perception of the home and then concentrate on how, along with practical suggestions on home improvements, the movement's concern with the domestic world of women led them to make political demands. I shall explore a wide variety of activities within the movement around the issue of housing; AGM resolutions, national surveys, essay competitions and the NFWI house at the Ideal Home exhibition. All of which enabled women to question the organisation of society and the power relationships within it that governed the material circumstances of their domestic lives. What I am arguing, therefore, is that the movement did not challenge women's association with domesticity – but that does not mean it was necessarily politically reactionary or that it accepted the status quo. The movement did question, challenge and re-negotiate the conditions under which women engaged in domestic work in a feminist way.

The NFWI motto 'For Home and Country' places the importance of the home at the centre of the movement's ideology and there was much sentimental poetry written by WI members elevating the home in the early years, for example:

> There is a dignity in labour.
> There is a sanctity in the home.
> For the mother at her washtub
> May see rainbows in the foam.
> And thoughts of her like lavender
> Allure the hearts that roam.[2]

The sanctity of the home was further developed as the typification of all that was English by W.R. Lethaby who wrote for *Home and Country* in 1923 praising the artistic qualities of the uncluttered English cottage and plain and simple furnishings. He says, 'The little cottages ... where they are kept in order and their dear little gardens, represent England more than any other things'.[3] Perceptions of the home as the heart of the nation, particularly the rural home in the light of the fears of racial deterioration at the turn of the century, were quickly adapted by the Movement. The rural home had been epitomised in World War One as an image of the England that soldiers were fighting for and many postcards from the front carried somewhat idealised pictures of rural cottages. At one level a concentration on domestic skills for women, housewifery and the significance of the home can be seen as part of a reactionary ideology. But this is too simplistic. The NFWI's stress on the importance of the home, as epitomised in their motto, had meaning for the membership. Acceptance or celebration of domesticity or domestic skills by the Women's Institute Movement must never be taken as an acceptance of the gender-power relationship, or material circumstances, within which they were predominantly carried out. Rather than accepted, these were areas which the movement sought to change and re-negotiate. Furthermore for those women past any point of choice about whether they would be housewives or not, elevation of the importance of the home and an emphasis on the site of reproduction rather than production was both validating and empowering. It offered them an alternative value system from which to challenge and re-negotiate structures of male power.

At the pragmatic level, local institutes particularly were involved in a number of handicraft activities to improve the physical surroundings of rural homes. Some were centred around repairs and maintenance, re-caning chairs, repairing and repainting furniture, for example. These skills were taught at regular institute meetings or in special classes put on at village or county level. Some of the handicrafts were about reviving old skills but many were oriented towards women being able to furnish their homes both cheaply and through their own intensive efforts; for example, making eiderdowns or patchwork quilts, making mattresses from oat flies, pillows from stripped oat feathers and a baby's cradle from a banana crate. There was an appeal to the membership in such items as they would last as a physical manifestation of the woman's domestic labour long after the more mundane tasks such as: cooking, washing and cleaning would have had to be done many times over. Also, women-produced material objects for the home were signifiers of women's productivity which contributed towards the creation of the home. They were not merely maintaining or servicing the home, which could be seen as provided out of the male wage packet. Home-made eiderdowns and patchwork quilts were signifiers of the rural women's independent contribution to the home. Through such activities the NFWI were able to challenge the meaning of women's domesticity. The house or home is not, therefore, for these women the site of female subservence, rather it was a site of domestic labour, of domestic production, which as the extract from the poem points out has a dignity of its own.

Domestic labour is not seen as intrinsically beneficial, labour-saving devices are always valued by NFWI members. A Lancing member writing in *Home and Country* in 1930 praises the reduction in the clothes babies wore, in babies' feeds and new materials for clothes as all bringing significant and positive changes in housewives' lives. While this member sees domestic work as always primarily the woman's responsibility, she is quite emphatic in her belief that domestic labour does not imply subservience saying 'Not masculine tyranny, not wifely submission, but this equal comradeship and the happy atmosphere are the real essentials of a lasting happy home'.[4] The movement was able to claim an authority and validity to demand social reforms to improve rural houses from: the ideological significance placed by the NFWI on the home, their identification of domestic labour as both skilled and of high status and their appropriation of notions of Englishness. Sometimes their requirements were a little vague and centred on the ideological as much as the pragmatic, for example in 1921 an AGM resolution was passed which stated that 'The NFWI should support any legislation to elevate and purify the home life of the nation'.[5] If rural homes were to be perceived as the heart of England and the traditional mothering and wifely role elevated, then, the NFWI members wanted the best material circumstances in which to fulfil these roles. Furthermore, if the nation wished to lay great emphasis on children as a national resource (which from the advent of New Liberalism at the beginning of the century it had done) the movement wanted the best possible conditions in which to bring children up. Many social commentators, at both ends of the political spectrum, in the first half of the twentieth century were keen to perceive the rural home as the embodiment of Englishness and the rural mother as the mother of the nation. The NFWI, therefore, turned this cultural association on its head to use it to their own advantage; to demand improvements in social services and the material conditions of their homes.

If, as Caroline Rowan has argued, the Women's Labour League and the Women's Co-op Guild through their campaigns around housing were 'opening up the home as a legitimate arena of political struggle'[6] for women in the towns, then the NFWI undoubtedly did the same for rural women. Campaigns around housing, water supplies and drainage could, in a real sense, operate to politically motivate women who might otherwise regard the political process as alienating. In a sense the personal may become truly political when women are involved in making political demands based on a desire to improve their own material circumstances in which they live and labour. The woman who had no piped water near her house and had to carry it all by hand and who sought to change this through combined action with other women was surely similar to male trade unionists who attempted to improve the conditions of their labour. For these women, issues were raised about why the local authorities and central government would not prioritise their demands and what they did prioritise instead. This could be politically enlightening. Before looking at the NFWI's involvement in housing campaigns in the period from 1918 until the 1950s, it is necessary to look at the wider situation with regards to state involvement in housing at the end of World War One within the context of debates around the role of social welfare.

In 1918 the rhetoric of 'Homes fit for Heroes' became a widely accepted political slogan throughout the country and a central part of the Government's post-war planning proposals. New homes were to be both a physical and ideological embodiment of the better future that was being fought for. The problem of housing was seen as being exaggerated by the rise in building costs expected (and realised) after the war. Furthermore, rent strikes in Glasgow and some other conurbations had placed housing centre stage in attempts to control the working class. However, the emphasis on housing was, arguably, seen mainly in urban terms as this was where the threat of working-class Bolshevism was considered strongest and also where fears of genetic deterioration of the race were focused. The 1919 Housing Act, while enabling local authorities to act and putting upon them a responsibility to do so, was open to very widely varying interpretation at local level. The implementation of the Act relied upon local councils' impetus which WIs tried to help along. Furthermore, the exact nature of houses to be built depended upon the local authorities presenting proposed schemes to regional housing directors for approval. But the Act did embody an important change. From 1919 until the Thatcher years the notion that the state had a responsibility for housing a significant proportion of the working class remained a consensual one.

The role of social welfare legislation such as housing can be seen in a number of different lights according to different historians's political perspectives. A crude Marxist interpretation could perceive it in terms of ensuring the maintenance of the capitalist system by buying off the working class. Alternatively, some feminists have seen the welfare state in post-war Britain as crucial in reproducing the subordinate position of women.[7] However, it is not necessary to embrace a Whig version of history in order to point out that welfare legislation has given at times both the working class and women some real material benefits. Welfare legislation is not, any more than anything else, open to a straightforward ideological reading; its meanings, its uses, the purposes it serves are different for different genders and social classes. Its introduction, implementation and practice are the result of struggle along class and gender lines. The level of Government intervention in the market economy is dependent on consensus support. This consensus, or consent, is a site of constant struggle and like any other area of hegemony it has to be constantly recreated or it can be lost, as recent years have indicated. Voluntary organisations like NFWI can also help build support for welfare measures, offer alternative and empowering interpretations of government provision and they can attempt to ensure that permissive legislation is enacted. From the 1919 Act onwards, housing and rural water supplies required just such activities in order really to improve the conditions of the rural working class. In all such areas the NFWI was to a degree active and I shall now return to looking at how.

The NFWI's first AGM in 1918 passed their first resolution on housing, stating:

> That the provision of a sufficient supply of convenient and sanitary houses being of vital importance to women in the country, County Federations and Women's Institutes are urged to bring pressure to bear upon their local councils and, through the National Federation, upon the Local Government board to ensure that full advantage is taken in their districts of the Government scheme for State-aided Housing.[8]

This resolution was ideal in that it provided a mandate for a wide variety of activities at local and national level within the movement in the following years. The NFWI were willing to join forces with other organisations in order to achieve improvements in housing. The 1918 annual report noted that the NFWI co-operated with the Rural Housing and Sanitation Association and the Women's Labour League on housing campaigns. Although there was some acceptance of the ideas of the Tudor Walters Report on Housing in 1918 that it was in the long term economic to build houses to a high standard, this was not always seen as possible. The aim was perceived to be a three bedroom house with a front and back garden, a separate parlour, hot and cold water in the house and a separate bathroom, not just a bath in the scullery. This was, however, only a recommendation and finances rarely allowed it. Where economies had to be made and what they were was subject to great debate in which the NFWI, like other women's organisations, participated. Another problem arose because the government insisted that economic rents be charged and to do so would ensure that the new council houses were rarely within the budget of a working-class family. In the immediate post-war period institutes gathered information on how many cottages were required by their village and why, the number of local people wanting cottages or imminently likely to and the number of local cottages needing rebuilding or repair. Thus the WIs were taking on the role of building a consensus in the village around the need for council houses and to ensure the implementation of the 1919 Act. Mrs Perkins of Bolder WI explained to *Home and Country* how her Institute had been asked if they had any special ideas to bring before the local council housing committee. Her optimism in the power of WI action was verbalised to other institutes thus:

> In places where the District Council and the Parish Council consider no cottages are wanted, probably helpful letters from the Women's Institute would convert them to better views, and in most cases they would welcome the interest taken. One of the difficulties in the past has been the indifference of the public to parochial affairs and the people themselves are to blame, not the Councils.[9]

The ideas or optimism of Mrs Perkins could be attributed to a liberal self-help ideology which, although it contains at times a plausible sense of reality which can be empowering, has many problems. It ignores the existence of power relationships within society and the very real conflicts of interest which operate upon gender, class and racial lines. Probably many working class NFWI members would not be able to ignore such conflicts of interest as they were so frequently on the wrong end of them.

Certainly, it took a little time for the members of the NFWI to realise that although perhaps helpful letters might deal with rural housing problems, probably they would not. In other areas councils were encouraged to hold a public exhibition of plans for any proposed council building in the village. Alternatively, in 1920 a writer in *Home and Country* pointed out that the Minister of Health had issued a circular (Circular 40) expressing the hope that all local authorities would take steps to obtain the views of women with regard to the proposed Housing Schemes.[10] This circular suggests plans should be shown to women's organisations or, where there is not one, a special meeting of village women should be called, and also that women should be co-opted onto housing committees. The intention was that after examination of the plans, village women could send in their suggestions to the housing committee of the council. As the article in *Home and Country* further argued, 'It is obvious that women who have to live and work and bring up their children in these houses know the requirements better than most men can possibly do'.[11] Institutes were encouraged to study the issues involved and appoint a special subcommittee to explore the subject of housing and to put Institute views to local councils. Once again in 1921 *Home and Country* set out clear instructions for action to be taken by Institutes:

> Members of a WI anxious to ensure that the cottages built in their own village should be well planned and arranged for the housewife can take action thus : they can decide which are the most essential points for them to urge and backed up by the Ministry of Health Circular 40, which recommends that plans should be exhibited before being adopted so that suggestions upon them by women can be received, they can apply to their rural District Council for the public display of plans.[12]

The demands of members were not by any means extravagant. Indeed, the ordinary members were encouraged by the leadership to work out and to express just what their requirements and priorities were. This very process encouraged them to perceive domestic labour and the material circumstances of their lives not as inevitable and fixed but as something constructed and not necessarily to their requirements. Such activities were essential in building up a consensus for government intervention and activity in the areas of housing and water supplies. They engendered in the members the possibility of change rather than an acceptance of the status quo. This could lead to members questioning why things were as they were and what they could do about it. One member described her ideal house for *Home and Country* thus:

An Essay by L.F. Boys Maidwell WI Northants
The House I Should Like to Live in

The house I should like to live in would be in the country, one cannot expect the same conveniences as in the town house.

I should like a double-fronted cottage with a nice sitting-room, a small hall and staircase, and a nice big airy kitchen with a good window, a dresser, cupboards and a range with a boiler, not necessary self-filling, for if the hard water tap or pump was in the scullery it would be quite easy to fill it.

I should like a nice-sized scullery, with a sink, a copper and a bath, as it would be quite easy to heat the water in the copper and not to have to carry it upstairs, and if there was a brick fireplace in the scullery where a kettle could be boiled in the summer when the range was not needed it would be very convenient. A nice airy larder, on the north side if possible. I should like to have three bedrooms with fireplaces and a nice garden in the front for flowers, a porch over the front door, so that I could grow a creeper to make it picturesque.

I should like also a coal house and a pig sty at the back, also a good-sized vegetable garden and a water closet if possible.[13]

In this fascinating mixture of the idyllic and the pragmatic it is important to note her requirements were well below the recommendations of the Tudor Walters committee. They were also dependent on the availability of piped water to her tap, which was a dream for many rural working-class housewives. Indeed *Home and Country* in the 1930s ran an essay competition for NFWI members on the problems of lack of village water.[14] Lack of piped water and sewage added tremendously to the burden of domestic labour any rural housewife had to undertake and therefore it was an area for agitation by the WI in rural areas. The demands for a water supply were seen as intrinsic to demands for improved rural housing and in 1935 the NFWI tried unsuccessfully to get an amendment to the Public Health Bill to stipulate that no new plans for houses should be passed without a water supply. The member's essay contains also a perception of the possibility of change as do the NFWI attempts to improve the rural water supply. Such a perception is an essential first step towards any political activity. It can be argued that one of the reasons that women tend to feel alienated from the political process is because they don't see it as in any way likely to change or alter their lives; this perception was something that NFWI membership and activities challenged. By making the home an area of political struggle the NFWI were able to politicise many rural women. Legislation on housing and on water and sewage was permissive. It gave local government the power to build council houses but did not compel them to do so or to take action to ensure that houses already in existence were brought up to an acceptable standard. Minimum suggested standards for such building and the approximate floor area were originally set in 1919 and reduced for economic reasons in the following years.[15] When the reductions came into force the result was, almost always, the elimination of the front parlour and the move to a house which contained a living room with a small scullery.

The reduction in rooms was limiting for the women who lived in the houses; it gave them little scope to carve out any space for themselves. It forced a situation whereby either the woman lived all the time in a room that was her workplace by using the living-room as a kitchen and the scullery only for limited messy work, or the scullery (a small room) became something like the small modern convenience kitchen built into many middle class semis of the period. Arguably, the small working kitchen owed a great deal to the middle-class cultural background of the architects and the consequent assumptions that domestic work (often carried out in the middle-classes by servants) should be unseen or invisible. To the working housewife what this did was to remove the centrality of her domestic role from the major living-room. Indeed, it could be argued that instead of the centre of the home being her domain in the kitchen/living-room and thus her dominating the home making it openly a site of domestic labour, she instead is placed in the back of the house, servicing the rest of the family. The parlour debate was heated and lengthy, with middle-class commentators arguing that it was merely a symbol of working-class pretentiousness and spent most of the time empty. However, it had numerous uses for: sick and elderly relatives, children's homework, for a little adult space away from children, not to speak of visitors. The NFWI remained firmly committed to the parlour principle, as did women generally. Despite this, by the 1930s no schemes for council house building which contained parlour-style houses were passed under the workings of the numerous and less generous Acts that had followed the 1919 Addison Act.

The NFWI executive were aware of their lack of knowledge on the reality of working-class women's homes, and one nervous working woman elected to the executive (referred to in chapter four) remembers Lady Denman assuring her that she had a valuable contribution to make, as most of the wealthy ladies on the executive did not know what went on behind cottage doors. Sure enough when they discussed housing she related how she was able to fill them in on the less picturesque elements of cottage living.[16] When the idealised images of country cottages espoused by some of the ruralist members of the leadership of the movement were given too much space, the membership was quick to respond. Thus when in 1926 Montague Fordham in an article entitled, 'Our Village – To-day, Yesterday and Tomorrow'[17] waxed lyrical about six hundred year old cottages and the importance of such cottages' relationship with nature and their surroundings (being built out of stone and wood) the membership were somewhat verbal. They criticised this perception of rural homes as typical of weekenders, 'not real country people' who wanted every modern convenience and labour saving device possible. The membership were critical and interactive when the leadership involved them in debates about homes. There was no blind acceptance of ruralist ideology.[18]

Indeed, it is the need to bridge the gap between the lived experience of the membership and the leadership which lay behind many NFWI surveys and questionnaires on housing and village life. They brought about a flow of information upwards to the rural élite and middle classes and acted to diffuse the reality of rural working-class living conditions through both different social classes and geographical areas of the movement. Furthermore, expressing complaints in this way helped to legitimise them. Once again the involvement by NFWI leadership, in exposing and campaigning against the worst housing conditions, helped make it clear that poor housing was not inevitable or merely to be put up with. It was then but a small step to the membership surmising that it was a Government responsibility to provide rural housing of a good standard. The questionnaire organised by the National Federation in 1942 should be seen in this light. Country Federations were asked to encourage local institutes to participate fully, preferably holding a meeting for the purpose. Forty-five of the counties returned results to central office. There were ten questions covering space allocation, garden size, storage, communal facilities, cooking and heating fuel, placement of housing, acceptable levels of rent, bathroom and WC arrangements as well as leaving space for local institutes' own suggestions. Participating in the questionnaire provided women with a space to explore their needs and verbalise their demands. A summary of these was published by the NFWI and was then was able to be used by the two NFWI members appointed to Government Committees on Housing, Mrs Methuen to the Rural Housing (Hobhouse) Committee and Mrs Haworth to the Design of Dwellings (Dudley) Committee. The summary points out:

> Many Institutes said they had never enjoyed anything so much. The house matters to a rural woman infinitely more than to a working man; she has to arrange it for her man and children: her knowledge is real, practical knowledge that counts. Here was a chance to give vent to pent-up feelings. Yet there are few extravagant suggestions. Neither is there any whisper of a suggestion that what was good enough for my mother is good enough for me.... Opinion may vary in detail on how to save labour and make cottage life more comfortable and more civilised. But two basic needs are emphasised in every reply – the need for an adequate water supply and the need for women architects and for working class women members on housing committees.[19]

This quote raises a variety of issues. Once again domestic women's skills and expertise were emphasised, both as a validation of what they had to say and as a reason for more female involvement in the planning process. This can be seen as reinforcing gender stereotyping but I do not think that is how the NFWI members saw it; rather the experience of partaking in the survey could be empowering. It was taking the cultural associations of women and domesticity and arguing for an improvement in women's working conditions. Indeed, there is a forceful emphasis in the writing that women have a right to material improvements in the conditions of their labour, for example in the reference that women were not prepared to accept the same circumstances as their mothers. An adequate water supply was seen, as ever, as a basic need. Questions about whether bathrooms and WCs should be separate seemed quite spurious to many Institutes from villages with no piped water. Other unanimous demands were for electricity, cupboards in every room and once again a parlour 'where children can do homework and friends can be entertained'. A quarter of an acre of garden was the most popular size and, although all preferred detached houses, most found semis acceptable, though not terraces.[20]

The NFWI concern with housing and water at this time was part of their thinking on post-war planning (which will be discussed in more detail in the next chapter) and it was a time when the radicalism always evident in NFWI ideology seemed at its most socialist. The 1943 AGM demanded:

> That this meeting is of the opinion that the three main services – water, sewage and electricity – should be a national responsibility, and that it should be possible to compel Local Authorities to take necessary action to ensure that adequate provision is made in the country as well as the town.[21]

This shows a significant shift in the expectation of the central Government's role and responsibility. Organisations like the NFWI were thus laying the groundwork in building a consensus around the concept of nationalisation of major services and a greater level of Government intervention in the housing market. In *Home and Country* in 1942 one writer wrote enthusiastically – 'It is obvious to everyone that post-war Britain is going to be very different. It needs to be. The best minds are agreed there must be more equality of opportunity, a fairer distribution of wealth, better homes for all'.[22] In July 1942, following local conferences on post-war housing in places like Chichester, the NFWI joined with other women's organisations to hold a conference on 'The House of our Dreams'. *Home and Country* reported, 'When an architect who presided suggested that sliding doors and drawers are expensive, a member said that if we could afford a war we could afford to save housewives' legs'.[23] The comment was indicative of a changing perception of what the Government was able to do. Perhaps women, having seen the huge level of Government expenditure undertaken in wartime, had became aware that Government spending is about priorities and choices and not just what can be afforded. Women were asserting their demand that their needs should be prioritised. Maybe at one level this does not seem like radical rhetoric and yet it is the words of women, slowly being empowered by the NFWI to believe that they can think in terms of change to their immediate environment. Debates raged within the movement as to the most desirable houses and how to ensure where they were built, also an important concern in view of the issues raised by planned villages, new towns and extending existing villages. The NFWI found it difficult to compromise with its diverse membership, as occurred when the Scott Report planned to use agricultural land for slum clearance projects. However, they felt able to encourage the refurbishment of old cottages. Their enthusiasm to see post-war house building taking place at some speed led to suggestions that this might be a possible area for ex-servicewomen to go into. Predictably, this did not meet with a large degree of support, especially from the relevant unions who wrote in *Home and Country* expressing their disapproval of such a plan.[24] Another source of debate became the question of who should design and build the houses.

In the early part of 1944, as part of the contestation over the design of rural housing and what constitutes 'adequate housing', Northamptonshire Federation of Women's Institutes organised a competition to design a pair of rural cottages. Architects sent in over 500 entries, reputed to be the largest number ever collected together in connection with rural housing. The conditions of the competition specified that the cottages should not exceed a total floor area of 1,000 square feet, were to be suited to a family of six and should be priced at such a level as was commensurate with council house building budgets. The prevalent NFWI stress on the significance of the separation of space was recommended to architects thus, 'While not wishing to tie the hands of competitors who may choose to put forward a different solution, in the promoters's experience this can best be achieved by providing for a kitchen/living-room, parlour or sitting-room, a wash-house or scullery and three bedrooms'.[25] The winning entry, by Mr P.M. Powell was particularly commended for meeting these stipulations and also showing concern for fuel conservation and providing what was described as a 'time and motion study kitchen' and, 'In the opinion of the promoters the winning designs show a greater understanding of the real needs of agricultural community than any of the ministry's designs so far produced. The facilities shown are a necessary minimum and have been planned to provide maximum efficiency'.[26]

However, in writing about the competition, the *Architects' Journal* applied totally different standards from those of the NFWI The architects saw the winning planned house as being well designed from the point of view of the male agricultural worker. It explained the merits of the winning entry thus:

> When he returns to his home he wants, first, somewhere to put his bicycle away, then a WC to use if he wants it. After that somewhere to shed his rain-soaked clothes and remove his dirty boots and generally clean himself up without disturbing his wife at work before entering his house proper. He would like to find this snug and warm, with a fire burning to welcome him and one which he knows is also doing at least one other job, possibly two, thereby filling him with the comforting feeling that he can afford it.[27]

Within this quote, the whole emphasis of good planning of a house is on how it is able to fit the needs and requirements of the male worker at the point of his return home from work, as if the household had to be organised around him instead of the rural housewife who spends most of her time within the home and for whom it is a place of work. With attitudes like that it is hardly surprising that the NFWI felt that women needed to be involved in all stages of the planning process!

To the NFWI executive, housing was to remain a topical concern for many more years; yet there are indications that its priority with members dropped, when the 1950 survey of amenities and public service was completed. Few NFWIs complained about slow or little house building. The writer of the report comments, 'This is a surprising feature of the return, but the lack of emphasis on housing may well reflect acceptance by institute opinion of a housing shortage in town and country alike, too general to constitute a specific village problem and too obvious to call for comment'.[28] I fear that the drop in the emphasis on house building may more specifically be an indication of the growing middle-class membership of the NFWI, particularly reflecting those who had moved out to the rural areas with the post-war spread of mains water and sewage. As yet the conflict between the new middle-class villagers (who saw the countryside principally as a place of recreation) and the rural working-class (who needed cheap accommodation) had not developed as it did in the latter post-war period when there was frequently a middle-class lack of support or downright opposition for rural council house building.

This potential conflict was perhaps held at bay in the early 1950s by the focus of the NFWI's attention in the area of housing being upon the Women's Institute House at the Ideal Home Exhibition.

In May 1950 the NFWI was approached by the *Daily Mail* to oversee the design of a house for the 1951 Ideal Home Exhibition.[29] The *Daily Mail* covered the costs not only for the architect and building but also for surveying members about plans. The house had to be within the current building regulations for a council house and was aimed at a similar cost. Lionel Brett was selected as the architect, but was by no means given his head. In terms of design his original brief came from the 1942 NFWI survey of members and it was their preferences and priorities that provided his restrictions. NFWI members were able to see their involvement with the Ideal Home Exhibition as a validation of the movement's expertise in relation to rural housing. It gave them a chance to realise, in a material form, the demands which had been formulating over the past thirty years about what constituted an ideal home. Not surprisingly local institutes were quick to incorporate a trip to the Ideal Home Exhibition into their 1951 programme.

A NFWI *ad hoc* committee was set up with Lady Brunner as chairman (*sic*). By June new questionnaires were on their way to all local WIs with a covering letter referring to the 1942 questionnaire. Members reported enthusiasm for it. They saw the Ideal Home Exhibition house as a chance to put their ideas into practice. The house was to be designed for a young family with three children. Based on the 1942 survey a series of guidelines were made about preferences, for example, the three room downstairs layout comprising; kitchen /living room, working scullery and a sitting room/parlour. It was to have: three bedrooms, two toilets, and an upstairs bathroom. Further tentative suggestions covered: the cooking facilities, solid fuel heating, outhouses, electricity, larders and a place for a pram inside the house. All local institutes were asked to find three volunteers, preferably the mothers of young children, to complete and return further forms which covered all manner of aspects of the house, floor coverings, paint or wallpaper and other specifics of the interior. This enabled the membership to feel closely identified with the exhibition house. By August nearly six thousand replies had been received which Gallup Polls summarised. The results were sent to the architect and following NFWI scrutiny of his draft, the final plans were in existence by the end of September. Then followed much work to choose the furnishings, once again influenced by the questionnaire but also by the members of the subcommittee who had a significant role as the arbiters of good taste. A *Home and Country* article described the decision-making process in connection with the house and the reasoning behind it. They argued that where they had chosen more expensive items these were 'well made designs' and that these designs would be cheaper if the wider public's taste could be cultivated to create a mass market for them. Here, there are again traces of the debate around good taste in the craft movement. Indeed, the house was full of examples of the movement's handicrafts; cot quilts, patchwork bedspreads and hand-painted furniture – all examples of practical items that NFWI members were encouraged to make to improve their home environment and of acceptable crafts. The combination of the new and the old are indicative of a new version of Englishness in relation to rural homes (which will be discussed more in the last chapter). Interestingly, one of the wallpapers they chose was a William Morris design. The house combined the political demands for improved material conditions in the home, such as hot and cold water and bathrooms, with the NFWI members' own individual skill and power to shape their environment. The article concluded by saying:

> William Morris wrote that men [*sic*] 'will discover, or rediscover rather, that the true secret of happiness lies in taking a genuine interest in all the details of daily life, in elevating them by art instead of handing them to unregarded drudges and ignoring them.'
>
> As we struggle with our inconvenient household arrangements, how often we would like to 'elevate' them, how often do we regard ourselves to be 'unregarded drudges'? But as WI members we have many opportunities of learning how to appreciate design and beauty. Besides demonstrating this the WI house also tries to show what fundamental standards of design and equipment would remove the drudgery from our 'Ideal Home'.[30]

This could at one level be read as trying to make a virtue out of the severe shortage of domestic servants in the post-war period, but it also ties in with the recurrent Women's Institute Movement theme of elevating housework to a skilled status and a potentially radical and empowering NFWI alternative female value system which redefines status and art so that they can be identified with female pursuits.

If the Ideal Home Exhibition house emphasised design and a more consumerist post-war version of housing, then the three winning NFWI essays for the 1953 Associated Countrywoman of the World Essay Competition entitled 'The Rural Home' portrayed the home as a site of domestic labour. The essays were written by a farmer's wife, a vicar's wife and a farmer's daughter (whose mother had died and who therefore carried out all the domestic labour in her household although still in her teens). It is interesting to note that all three were functioning within a home seen as a focus of male working lives as well as their own. All were keeping house in some way not merely for themselves but for a male, be he father or husband. All three enthused over whatever modern improvements their houses had – water, electricity, modern electric or solid fuel cookers, bottled gas, a coke boiler and a telephone in the vicarage. Yet these essays did not in anyway celebrate consumerism, but rather practicality. However, there was a resigned stoicism about other less than ideal areas. 'The roof of the house leaks and nobody seems to be able to repair it, so we have a wonderful collection of tins and pots and pans in the attic in which rain water collects and is then guided into a funnel through which it drops rather noisily onto the landing'.[31] Or, 'I wish we had a telephone but daddy says that would be an expensive toy'.[32] All the essays laid positive emphasis on the home as a centre of family life. All the homes were old and notions of tradition and Englishness pervaded which incorporated the modern cookers and other equipment rather than in any way being displaced by them. What also came across in these essays is their role as rural housewives and their perception of its tradition and significance to the nation which was empowering and provided them with a sense of assurance and, backed by the movement's alternative value system, a sense of confidence. Hence a female role which may appear to be reactionary and submissive could, through contestation over meaning, provide women with a space to combat the internalisation of their oppression.

Despite NFWI pressure, both nationally and locally, it was clear in 1956 that women were still not having a say in the design of council houses in rural areas and yet were frequently living with the consequences of this omission. The 1956 survey of amenities in rural area carried out by the NFWI and reported in 'Our Villages' demonstrated this. A few examples give a sense of the tone:

> It is hard to credit that wash houses can be built without water (hot or cold), without ventilation, with no daylight except from the open door, and no electric light or power plug although the house is on mains water

and main electricity. Yet eight county Federations report such a wash house ... the connection between a wash-house and water would seem to be more a matter of normal intelligence than sex.[33]

Such examples are numerous. West Suffolk and Essex reported larders next to the hot tank. There is a piteous lament from the mining villages who find expensive electricity installed for cooking and heating and only one open fire on which to use their concessionary coal. Many more counties lament the lack of mains water and sanitation in council houses built in the 1950s and:

> Shropshire writes of houses for old people where the bath is upstairs and the water has to be carried up in buckets.
> Other Hampshire housewives suffer from airing cupboards at the top of the stairs – 'one step back and down you go'. Small matters these but galling to the occupant, and all might have been avoided by a little imagination on the part of the architect.[34]

All comments are indicative of NFWI members as consumers and as dissatisfied ones at that. They are once again emphasising the gap in cultural and practical experience between the designers and the consumers of much modern housing. The slightly humorous tone is a foretaste of the women's consumer programmes of the 1970s and 1980s but also a female subcultural affirmation of male incompetence and ignorance about the practicalities of life and these women's area of skill – the rural home. The representation of the work of people in power, or at least operating in some form of authority, as ridiculous and humorous serves to undermine their power. The official role of county planners and architects is delegitimised by the tone of the 'Our Villages' pamphlet. Once again the Women's Institute Movement could be seen to be chipping away at dominant power relationships and be empowering for women.

The NFWI's emphasis on the home, housing conditions and water supplies were a natural extension of their motto 'For Home and Country' and reflected the predominantly domestic orientation of the membership. Their domestic orientation was based within an alternative female value system, which they were able to develop as an all women's group. Therefore, as I have shown, this did not lead to a reactionary political position, but rather they reworked ideas of the national importance of the home to empower them and demand social welfare reforms. For rural women in the NFWI, agitation around the home as the site of their labour was as significant in raising their political consciousness as men's demands to improve the conditions of their labour within the trade union movement. Many of their demands, such as for water supplies to rural areas, came to be realised in time, but it is hard to estimate what level of direct responsibility they can take for this. I would like to argue that they were significant in helping to build a consensus for the necessity of certain standards of rural housing and water supplies. They were a site for the contestation of definitions of adequate housing. Even disregarding this, maybe the importance for NFWI members in campaigns for social reforms, of which housing was only one, is more complex and tied up with challenging perceptions of themselves and femininity. Mike Thompson has argued:

> It is important that people's consciousness changes through direct involvement in bringing about change. It is not the reform or the concession itself which is important, but the understanding that stepping outside the normal feeling of futility and passivity is effective. If people learn that they can influence the course of events, particularly if they step outside the traditional methods of doing so, then limited community action is worth while.[35]

In this light the NFWI activities around housing can be seen as significant because they implied to members the potential for change, for their own actions to influence the decision-making process. In both the surveys and the case of the Ideal Home Exhibition house their demands and dreams were given concrete expression. Campaigns for welfare provision were, therefore, another area in which members were able to re-negotiate the boundaries of their femininity and challenge their own internalisation of the socially constructed subservience of women. As such they could be a significant site of feminist activity. It is now necessary to return to a more specific historical period and explore how the Women's Institute Movement's feminism was able to survive and thrive within wartime – when it might be perceived that machismo was privileged.

NOTES

1. *Keeping Ourselves Informed*, NFWI publication, London 1981, p132.
2. *Home and Country*, May 1923, p14.

3. *Home and Country*, March 1923, p19.
4. *Home and Country*, October 1930, p516.
5. 1921 annual report, p29.
6. C. Rowan, 'Women in the Labour Party', in *Feminist Review 12*, 1982, p89.
7. Elizabeth Wilson, *Women and the Welfare State*, Tavistock, London 1977.
8. *Keeping Ourselves Informed*, NFWI publication, London 1981, p137. 10, 1918 NFWI annual report, p67.
9. *Home and Country*, April 1919, p13.
10. *Home and Country*, May 1920, p7.
11. *ibid.*
12. *Home and Country*, Febuary 1921, p15.
13. *Home and Country*, December 1919, p12.
14. *Home and Country*, April 1932, p146.
15. Mark Swenarton, *Homes fit for Heroes*, Heinemann, London 1981.
16. Mrs Freeman, oral testimony (5) typed and kept in History file in NFWI archive.
17. *Home and Country*, April 1926, p6.
18. *Home and Country*, July 1926, p18.
19. Summary of answers to rural housing questionaire in Housing file in NFWI archive.
20. Evidence for the Central housing Advisory Committee's subcommittee on the Design of Dwellings – in Housing File of the NFWI archive.
21. *Keeping Ourselves Informed*, NFWI publication, London 1981, p132.
22. *Home and Country*, May 1942, p87.
23. *Home and Country*, July 1942, p104.
24. *Home and Country*, July 1944, p103.
25. 'Northamptonshire Federation of Women's Institutes Housing Competition' in NFWI archive, p1.
26. *ibid.*, p2.
27. *Architect's Journal*, 30 March 1944, reprinted in 'Norhampton Federation of Women's Institutes Housing Competition', NFWI pamphlet, London 1944, in NFWI archive.
28. 'Survey of Amenities and Public Services', 1950, an NFWI pamphlet, in NFWI publications file in NFWI archive.
29. This and much of what follows is based on the Ideal Home Exhibition File in the NFWI archive.
30. *Home and Country*, March 1951, p71.
31. *Home and Country*, February 1953, p41.
32. *Home and Country*, March 1953, p81.
33. Cecily McCall, 'Our Villages', NFWI pamphlets, 1956, in publications file in the NFWI archive.
34. *ibid.*, p5.
35. M. Thompson (ed), *Community Organising*, Macmillan, London 1982, p214.

6

WAR YEARS

In 1940 there was, in the gardens of England, a nationwide glut of plums which, apparently immune to the attentions of thieving boys or more legitimate consumers, threatened to rot on the ground. Such a waste in a time of food shortage was apparently averted by the stalwart efforts of Women's Institute Movement jam-makers. Jam-making, so the story goes, through a fluke of nature was to become the NFWI contribution to the war effort. Cecily McCall, a NFWI employee summed up the appeal of jam-making in 1943:

> Jam-making was constructive and non-militant, if you liked to look at it that way. It accorded with the best Quaker traditions of feeding blockaded nations. For those who were dietetically minded, jam contained all the most highly prized vitamins. For those who were agriculturally minded the scheme saved a valuable crop from literally rotting on the ground, and it encouraged better fruit cultivation – though not, one can only pray, of plums only. And for the belligerent, what could be more satisfying than fiercely stirring the cauldrons of boiling jam and feeling that every pound took us one step further towards defeating Hitler.[1]

What could be more reassuring and unchallenging than the image of numerous elderly ladies in pinnies, no doubt, making pounds of jam in kitchens and village halls with a patriotic fervour ? It fits in perfectly with a certain version of England at war, embodied, perhaps also at times, by Ealing cinema. And it is an image which the Women's Institute Movement has suffered from ever since. The association between jam-making and the NFWI has become part of our common cultural currency. However this was only a small facet of institute activities during the war years. Pre-war the Women's Institute Movement had become a focus for women-centred and controlled leisure in the villages, whist drives, socials, summer fairs, drama, folk-dancing, singing and the yearly outing for the members. All this they continued to organise, though the outing could be in a horse and cart rather than a coach. Indeed institute membership could be a many faceted experience in wartime, on the practical side this included food production and preservation 'make do and mend', sewing circles, knitting clubs, helping at WI markets, lining coats with fur for Russia, distributing meat pies to agricultural workers, and organising or cooking school dinners. There was also the building of 'the new Jerusalem'. Despite such problems as the evacuation of the NFWI headquarters and paper shortages affecting the length of *Home and Country*, they were heavily involved in discussing the planning of post-war Britain. They continued to campaign for social welfare legislation, demanding equal compensation for men and women's war injuries, and they supported the increases in agricultural workers wages. Within this chapter, I will concentrate on the following themes: how the movement adapted to wartime, its role in wartime food production and domestic economy, the evacuation scheme and the role of the NFWI in giving a voice to the foster mothers and post – war planning. It is my argument that these areas highlight both the continuity of the NFWI' s version of feminism and Englishness of the 1930s but also changes and reworkings, particularly around the ideology of domesticity, foregrounded by the national concern with the Home Front during World War Two.

It is necessary first to look at the movement's position with regard to war in the 1930s, which set the boundaries of its wartime activities. The NFWI was by its constitution allowed to discuss no matter which was party political or denominational. It was to be an organisation which women of any religion or political party felt comfortable to join. Therefore no action which could be perceived as preparation for war, or assisting in anyway towards armed combat, was sanctioned by the NFWI in the interests of Quaker members. It can be argued that organisations like the NFWI, and the Women's Co-operative Guild who would not directly support the war effort, lost out badly in terms of membership to the Women's Voluntary Service (WVS). I think that rather more significant in membership terms was the loss of young women from the rural areas to the forces and town-based munitions work. This was to a degree counteracted by the arrival of Land girls. The Land Army had close links with the NFWI, in terms of organisational leadership at least, Lady Denman being both NFWI Chairperson and the Director of The Land Army. Although links were encouraged between the organisations at a local level, it is likely that it was the war period which generally speaking estranged the movement from young single women. Certainly the NFWI, along with many other feminist organisations in the 1920s and 1930s, was involved in peace work. A real sense of the horror of war, which is a legacy of this, comes across in the response to a letter in *Home and Country* which had described the bliss one woman felt at spring in wartime. The correspondent argues, 'When she watches an air battle, and feels she has done it herself , does she think of the young men killed, maimed, trapped in burning wreckage? British or German they are all mothers' sons'.[2]

In the early days of the phoney war, the uncertainty about a suitable role for the organisation resulted in a large amount of rhetoric and a familiar wartime theme that the spirit of Englishness, a version of which the NFWI was seen as embodying, was as important a weapon as spitfires and bombers.[3] For example, Lady Denman's first message of the war to the institutes included the following words:

> In the first place everyone of us can help to keep alive a spirit of steadiness and freedom of panic. Germany is said to count on breaking our nerve. Every person who spreads an atmosphere of cheerfulness and quiet resolution at this time is helping to win the war. We are proud of the cause for which Britain is fighting.[4]

The 'cause' is obviously in a sense a construct. Wars are about antagonism between nations and nationhood itself is a cultural construct embodying ideas of tradition, history and heritage. Without this, a nation is but arbitrary lines on a map, although nationhood must be constantly recreated and re-negotiated. Wartime necessitates a version of Englishness which is constructed against the enemy as other. In World War Two one of these constructs was of cowardly Germans compared to brave little Britain. This version of Englishness incorporated a spirit of fortitude and pluckiness, which was to deal with the danger of war by almost pretending it wasn't happening, by carrying on as normal, by implying there was nothing to fear, hence an image of the English gaily singing in the air-raid shelters. The large numbers of the population who after the first bombings on Coventry, with straightforward common-sense, fled to the surrounding areas adhered to a different version of reality.[5] However, an image of the English stoically, with some jollity even, carrying on their everyday life in the face of war is still a potent one, both during and after the war. Thus the English at one level could win the war by carrying on as normal, by simultaneously undertaking huge changes in their lives and also pretending nothing untoward was happening. Thus the twin themes of continuity and change were held together in a version of English everyday life. A local WI monthly meeting was a prime site for this contradictory ideology to operate. Lady Denman, again, says, 'keep the social side of the WI alive however hard this may be even if our usual generous tea has become only a cup of tea and a biscuit'.[6] Within this complex mixture of ideas the following report, by a NFWI demonstrator in West Sussex, and the development of similar myths must be seen:

> I went to B. to speak and arrived three minutes before two high explosive bombs threw up enormous quantities of sticky red mud, which smothered me from head to foot, but as all the members were smothered likewise or with plaster from the ceiling it didn't seem to matter much and I have never demonstrated better.[7]

Within this story, or myth, lies a version of the England that is being fought for – women who would not be deterred from the day-to-day matter of a WI meeting and demonstration by the little matter of an incendiary bomb. However, Englishness is a contested construct and attempting to read versions of it from texts available or from people's memories is a practice fraught with difficulties and uncertainties, furthermore it remains uncertain how accepted such versions of Englishness were. E.M. Delafield (a Women's Institute VCO herself) describes in her fictionalised *Diary of a Provincial Lady* the discussion at start of the war over the continuance of WI meetings:

> Doubt has been cast on the possibility of continuing WI monthly meetings but this is dispersed by announcement, said to have come from Lord Privy Seal, no less, that they are to be continued. Mrs F from the mill – our secretary has undertaken to inform all members that the Lord Privy Seal says that we are to go right on with our meetings just the same and so it will be all right.[8]

This could, however, be read as an indication of the nervousness, in the changed circumstances of war, that women felt about their right to time and leisure for themselves that they had managed to achieve in WI meetings. Whatever the notion of everything as normal one letter to *Home and Country* pointed out:

Of course we all know the difficulties are enormous. Life in the reception areas is not all blackberrying nor wholly knitted squares. One Government department tells us to double our activities for the doubled rural population, another seizes our halls. (No ill feeling just war time) County Federations beg us to meet before dark; school shifts fill up the rooms till 5:30.[9]

Despite the practical difficulties of finding halls and the demands on rural women's time as a result of hosting evacuees, most local WIs continued to meet monthly for their social and educational meeting, usually in the afternoon because of the blackout. In 1941 a *Home and Country* editorial claimed:

There is no doubt that in the dark days of 1940s perfect summer, when the nation was confronted with one disaster after another, the quiet customary functioning of the WI's was an important factor in the villages the maintenance of morale that never waived.[10]

Some institute activities were out of the ordinary – 'one offs'. An unusual example of this occurred in Angmering, West Sussex just before the second front, when Brenda McBride, and other Queen Alexandra's nurses billeted in the village were issued with their kit. She describes it thus:

The kit issue was depressing. It consisted simply of regulation men's khaki battle dress trousers and jacket but treated with chemicals to repel vermin, particularly body lice. In addition the outfit had been designed for men. The unyielding trousers were too tight over the behind too big around the waist and too long in the waist except for giraffes like Miss Agate. It was time someone informed the war office of the difference between men and women.

Mr Cummings the butcher found us trying on our new uniforms. Margaret Anderson was standing in barrel-like trousers which fitted the hips but left enough room at the waist for another QA, 'I'll fetch the wife' he spluttered as he rushed off.

Mrs Cummings was a tower of strength. With the aid of the Women's Institute sewing circle, the Sock group and the Balaclava bee she converted our AVs from fancy dress into a wearable uniform.

We looked almost soldierly except for the burgeoning breast pockets and something aggressive about the seat of the pants.[11]

In this there is once again something of a loose attitude to the interpretation of what is defined as 'helping prepare for war'. A desire to help other women, with the common female concern of physical appearance, here overrides the ethical issues raised by the fact it was airforce uniform, at least within this institute. This was a straight forward practical task. There was, none the less, considered to be something of a tension about getting the balance of emphasis within institutes right – between practical activities in relation to the war or building morale which was discussed. In 1941 a playlet was published in *Home and Country* which focussed on a dialogue between the mother and auntie of young Albert. They both belong to different institutes which have rather different priorities. Auntie explains:

> Our President said there's two kinds of things the institute can do for the country the things you can see and touch and the things you can feel in your bones. And both are going to last and help the country after the war.

she continues:

> I feel in my bones that we're going to win this war, and that we're going to make the world a better place to live in when its over. The institute has helped me to think that. We've kept up our choir and our drama team so as to give the village a bit of entertainment now no one can get into town much.[12]

Mum continues to be put right. When she admits to indulging in the time honoured practice of taking a nap when the last NFWI speaker came down, she is reprimanded. 'This one was a bit different she said something I can't forget. She said its a splendid thing if your institute is a fruit preservation centre but see you make it a mind preservation centre'.[13] However despite the Women's Institute Movement's federal structure, different institutes placed different emphasis on different areas of activity. Though in popular memory, it is the fruit preservation, rather than mind preservation, for which the NFWI was known, although the WVS also ran jam centres.

Food production and preservation was first put high on the agenda in 1938 when the NFWI was approached by the Government to encourage domestic food production in times of peace and war. By the 1930s the agricultural side of the movement was severely diminished. It could more accurately be described as cottage farming, that is the growing of vegetables and keeping of small animals in cottage gardens and allotments which was able to contribute to the rural women's independence. It took the threat of war, and therefore food production moving up the national agenda, for it to become as major a concern within the movement and in 1939 the NFWI set up the Produce Guild,[14] with a Government grant to pay for a full-time organiser, her travel costs and some other running costs. The aim of the guild was to encourage the production of food and the best use and preservation of home-grown food. Membership was open to any NFWI member with an annual subscription of one shilling, (felt by some at the time to be prohibitively high). The guild was run on county lines and there was a food production section and a use and preservation of home-grown produce section. These sections were subdivided under headings such as bee-keeping, poultry, milking, dried vegetables, chutney and pickles. Like the NFWI Guild of Learners, which already existed, the Produce Guild ran tests at four levels – a work test, a demonstrator's test, a teacher's test and a judge's test referring to particular specialities of the already mentioned sections. On passing a work test the Produce Guild badge could be worn. The very name Produce Guild and the test system together served to raise food production, as practised by housewives, to a skilled status; as the Guild of Learners had done for craftwork within the movement. The Produce Guild covered a wide variety of areas. In 1942 in Breconshire WI volunteers planted potatoes on 130 acres of reclaimed land at the top of a mountain. Seeds were supplied through the Produce Guild for the growing of onions, shallots, tomatoes and, of course, potato cultivation was encouraged. The collection and drying of herbs for medicinal purposes was also undertaken and the Guild trained interested members in canteen and community cookery. The do's and don'ts of keeping chickens, especially with the shortage of ordinary foodstuffs, were documented in *Home and Country* under a series entitled 'Betty in the Hen House'. Rabbits were strongly encouraged for meat and fur, goats for butter, milk and cheese, bees for honey. In 1941 the *Home and Country* editorial in January claimed that:

> This year's special contribution by WI's to national life and effort will be as it was last year through the production and preservation of food. The aim of every village was to be self supporting in vegetables and to run pig clubs.[15]

Recipes for rationing were distributed, such as potato rock cakes and scones from porridge. Problems arose in home-made jam and marmalade manufacture because of sugar rationing, particularly when in 1941 the Government decided not to provide an extra ration of sugar for home jam-making as it had the previous year. Citric acid and vinegar were advised to help set the jam, and apple windfalls could be included in almost anything along with vegetables which were seen as lending colour and bulk, whereas, grated carrot was apparently indistinguishable from orange peel in marmalade. Members did not receive suggestions uncritically; there was much disquiet over a recipe for curing ham in 1944. The majority of members, it was pointed out, had not seen hide nor hair of a ham for some time.

In 1940 the first jamming and fruit preservation centres opened at the request of the Minister of Agriculture and with the Government's financial assistance. This covered loans for setting up centres, as well as assurances to underwrite potential financial losses and the provision of permits for sugar for the scheme. The jamming centres operated one or two days a week during the season in village halls, outhouses of large houses, members' kitchens or a mobile unit. Fruit was donated or bought, or brought to be preserved. The schemes were based to some extent on the co-operative jam centres in Norfolk in the 1920s and instructions were quite specific. For example, in 1941 they made clear:

> All work must be done co-operatively. No county federation nor the NFWI may give permission for sugar to be sold or distributed for domestic production. Jams, jellies, fruit cheeses, chutneys, fruit syrups, canned or bottled fruits may be made with centre sugar, marmalade, mincemeat, home made wines, cider or perry may not be made.[16]

In 1940 it was estimated that 1,170 tons of fruit that would otherwise have been wasted was saved. Jam was examined and graded by NFWI judges and had to be made to Ministry of Agriculture recipes and proportions. Distribution of the jam and other preserves was not after 1942, even slightly, at the discretion of the centre. It had to go to hospitals, institutions, canteens or shops which sold it for ration points. It galled some of the women that they worked long hours for no pay, in questionable conditions and that they could receive none of the jam, hence the strength of feeling that lay behind the following report in *Home and Country* in 1944:

Preservation centres may like to know that the NFWI press department took immediate action on the paragraph which appeared in the *Daily Mail* on Thursday the 11 May which stated that 540 tons of institute jam was still on grocers' shelves and that the public would not buy it. It appears that some wrong information was given to the reporter by an irresponsible grocer in a London shop. The statement that the jam in question was made by the WIs was a mistake as the varieties were dried peach and rhubarb.[17]

Participation in fruit preservation centres could be, for members, a further validation that their domestic labour – in a preservation centre one day in their own kitchen the next – was of national importance. For some members however, storage was a problem, Langton Maltravers WI war history recounts:

> Three depots of jam were organised by the Women's Institute. In those strange days, when parachutists were expected by day and night a serious problem arose. Was it wiser to hide one's store of jam under the floor or somehow sealed up in a quarry hole or was it better to imitate a Jael housewife who kept a hammer ready for a last minute smashing, in the hopes of the dire effects of powdered glass on jam-starved Germans.[18]

Obviously, if the English had jam, the Germans must have none. From jam-making being perceived as of national importance, it became the embodiment of Englishness itself and therefore under threat from a German invasion. However although 2,600 village centres worked in 1940 and 4,500 registered in 1941, by May 1942 only 3,366 centres had registered. 284 refused to operate again, worn down by the effort, the demands on their time and much ministerial red tape.

Canning centres operated in a similar way, with canning machines sometimes supplied by the county federation or sent from Canada. Other equipment was often rudimentary and some such as Fishbourne in West Sussex, did all the fruit preparation outside in fine weather. They often brought their own equipment although there seems to have been no compunction about buying extra large pans, to boil the fruit in, on the black market. One mother of five described to me how after taking her eldest four children to school, she put her youngest in the pushchair and loaded on to it a packed lunch, colanders, wooden spoons and pans and walked over two miles, twice a week, to help at a canning centre.[19] There were several processes involved in canning: sterilisation, grading, packing, making syrup, sealing cans, labelling and picking over. The group had to attend a course and pass, with a certificate being awarded, to indicate they had reached an adequate level of competence. The canning machine required a high level of skill and precision one women recalled it thus:

> You had to turn the handle and it had to be in neutral to start with and this is what caused so many problems. It had to be absolutely neutral to start with and it had to be turned exactly twenty times ... I fell into it quite easily the other four kept on having trouble with it.[20]

The cans had to meet standards and were inspected by NFWI judges, the precision was important because faulty cans could explode rather dramatically. The group were paid to can for people or were given excess fruit and then had to sell the cans in the same way as the NFWI jam. Once again the emphasis on skill and the elevation of a domestic task to national significance was important, but surely there were other issues at stake. These preservation centres, as well as sewing circles, make and mend clubs, provided (as ordinary WI meeting always had) a women's support network during wartime. Such women's activities were significant for confidence-raising, and helped to challenge dominant perceptions of femininity. Women's ability to do things when men are not present, their discovery of a different atmosphere, confidence and relaxation, tends to lead to a questioning of what it is and how it is that they are not normally able to behave in such ways in the presence of men. This ties in, I think, with the support and consciousness-raising Nella Last gets from the WVS centres in *The Nella Last Diaries*[21] in the Mass-Observation archives, or my own memories as a child of my own grandmother recounting gleefully stories of her wartime work with groups of women rolling bandages and knitting balaclava helmets. *Home and Country* frequently carries humorous accounts of such events, particularly in a series entitled 'Miss Toomb's Jottings' which seem to take on board these reasons for WI members' involvement in such activities.

One final area that the movement's concern with feeding the nation moved into was school dinners, which is worth mentioning because it is a precursor of the provisions of the post-war welfare state. Local authorities had been permitted to provide school dinners since 1906 and 1926 and 1939 NFWI resolutions supported their introduction. In the 1930s the number that actually did so steadily reduced. During the war the NFWI campaigned for the widespread provision of school meals and in some areas arranged the cooking of them. This was seen as advantageous for the children in nutritional terms, and an article in *Home and Country* in 1939 had strongly encouraged mothers to ensure that, even if they were more expensive, to try and utilise school meals where possible. The National Federation provided a booklet on school dinners to help advise members on what an adequate school dinner should comprise of and how to campaign for their implementation. Following evacuation many more institutes became involved in the issue of school meals, as it was potentially a real saving in their domestic labour. Both these issues are reflected in their 1943 AGM resolution which states:

> That this meeting whilst appreciating the progress which has been made in the School Meals Scheme, notes that there are still many schools without canteens, and urges; (1) Local Education Authorities to accelerate their arrangements (which should not be wholly dependent on voluntary effort) so that all schools may be served; (2) parents to take full advantage of such provision where it exists.[22]

The 1944 Education Act required all local authorities to provide a mid-day meal in all maintained schools.

Women's domestic economy skills which were not linked to food production also took on national significance. The NFWI's tradition of exhibitions and competitions which gave craft a public status, focused on such wartime crafts as make-do-and-mend. One interviewee told me with great enthusiasm about a pair of make and mend trousers she had made during the war, out of a velour jacket and an old shirt of her husband's. These trousers had gone all the way up through the NFWI structure to an exhibition in London. She was extremely proud of these trousers, although as she herself pointed out her son wore through the knees of them in no time at all, just like any other pair.[23] Indeed this comment of hers indicates perhaps why the NFWI members adopted so eagerly, it seems, the idea of validating their work through various judging systems exterior to their home. Much domestic labour involves merely the unending toil to return things to the status quo of the day before, with no obvious product to show. People may be fed, houses may be clean, but the dirt and the requirement for food will be there again the next day. Winning competitions, having trousers placed in exhibitions, making numerous pounds of jam in a preservation centre leaves some sort of record of a domestic women's productiveness, as the weekly wage has recorded a man's productivity – even if it is consumed by the end of the week. That housework should be recognised as productive and regarded as a skilled profession is a re-occurring theme amongst NFWI and other post – suffrage feminists, right through to the 1970s wages for housework campaigns. Such women did not want to reject the domestic sphere but to re-negotiate its boundaries and challenge its low status. From a position of 1990s feminism, it is still possible to see the radical connotations of their struggles. Domestic work, within a male-dominated capitalist society, is a low status occupation, because it is a primarily a female sphere and because it is not evaluated by the marketplace. Women can, through alternative female cultures and value systems, challenge the low status of domestic labour. They can prioritise it and legitimate its value and thus challenge their own internalisation of subservience. Indeed, this notion of feminism, as essentially about raising the status of housework, is present in an article in *Home and Country* in 1941 entitled 'The Nation's Cinderella'. Feminism was described as having two strands, firstly to improve the political position of women which is seen as having had some success, and a much slower improvement is seen as occurring in the second area, which is:

> To show that women doing their own traditional and specific job of running a household and bringing up a family should be considered as important, as responsible and as much worthy of respect as women doing the kind of job that can be done equally well by either sex; and that their work is just as vital if not more so.[24]

Thus within an organisation like the NFWI there was a continuity in accepting a primarily domestic role for women, but the meaning and status of this role was constantly challenged. In World War Two the Home Front was itself elevated to national significance. It became an example of, to quote Patrick Wright, 'The rags and tatters of everyday life taking on the lustre of the idealised nation when touched by its symbolism'.[25] What had been for women everyday tasks, became within wartime, of national importance. Thus: Dig for Victory, Make-do-and-Mend, the importance of the patriotic potato and the existence of the Produce Guild all served to help women challenge their internalisation of the low status of domesticity. Consequently they allowed for some reworking, renegotiation and contestation over the social construction of domesticity and femininity. If these areas helped to raise women's status, then the evacuation schemes resulted in many rural women feeling exploited and alienated by the Government's actions, and the NFWI became one of the few areas in which they could express their views.

Evacuation was something that touched the majority of rural areas in which Women's Institutes operated, although some rural areas on the South Coast went from being reception areas to being evacuated themselves. Many NFWI members were at the forefront of receiving evacuees and the NFWI was one of the few organisations through which the host women could verbalise their grievances over what, in retrospect, can be seen as one of the administrative messes of all time. This is despite the planning that went on for it from the 1920s onwards. Indeed, prior to war the NFWI had carried out a survey of the homes of sixteen million people and in November 1938 following the Munich crisis, they presented suggestions about how any proposed evacuation should take place.[26] They were critical of the plans that existed at the time as unworkable, and suggested children from two to five should be in nursery or crêche units containing at least ten children, with specialised staff or foster mothers. They pointed to the need for after school activities for older children and warned against the resentment indiscriminate billeting would cause. Finally, they pointed out that the formula of one person to one room was biased in favour of those with larger houses and much larger rooms. Thus even before evacuation was put into place the NFWI, in the interest of their members, took on the role of representing its problems.

Whatever the bias in their favour, many middle-class women were horrified at the prospect the indiscriminate billeting of working class children on them, and many like the heroine in *Diary of a Provincial Lady* hurriedly acquired distant relations and friends to fill empty rooms.[27] The middle classes had a fear of evacuation which, as well as pure class prejudice, amounted to a recognition of the potential domestic labour involved and their inadequacy to carry out the unfamiliar tasks involved in such work. In 1939 E.M. Delafield says of evacuation:

> In the type of home in which all or most of the domestic work is usually done by one, two or three maids this will be a definite problem and it ought to be considered now, as part of the national service that all are

anxious to render. It has been for a long while, as we all know, very
difficult to get domestic workers to remain in country places. It is going
to be much more difficult, when everything is disorganised by a national
emergency, when new and exciting jobs are springing into being, and
when conditions under which such work as cooking and cleaning are to
be done are bound to be more difficult and less clearly done than in
normal times.[28]

In Delafield's *Diary of a Provincial Lady* a rota of local WI members
helped the maidless vicar's wife cope with the domestic labour created
by numerous evacuees billeted on the vicarage.[29] Domestic labour was
not the only reason that there was resentment towards evacuees. The
cultural construction of the rural home as the heart of the nation
(mentioned in previous chapters) also had its part to play. The legacy
of the back-to-the-landism popular with both the political right and
the left at the turn of the century had mixed with Baldwin's version of
Englishness in the 1920s and 1930s. This had enabled rural women to
think of themselves as ideologically speaking for the mothers of the
nation. Indeed in 1939 Walter Elliot, Minister of Health, told the
NFWI AGM:

> The land is the mother of us all, but the members of the Women's
> Institute are the mothers of the land. Here we have the wives and
> daughters of the farmers of England and Wales, who are people who
> have really made the land of England and Wales in thousands of years in
> patient toil.[30]

It does not matter that very few of the Women's Institute Movement
were in actuality related to farmers, their constituency was, in reality,
much wider than that. The association of ruralism and rural women
with Englishness and their role as the guardians of a tradition, of a way
of life, was by the 1940s ingrained. Although neither tradition nor
Englishness were fixed concepts, these rural women saw themselves as
the essence of English womanhood, indeed, it was embedded in their
identity. A sense of identity was created through boundaries, through
difference and against what was identified as Other. And this Other,
their ideological opposite, was a town way of life, a town version of
domesticity, of motherhood and womanhood. What was then,
predictably, bound to happen when this other way of life, which they
defined themselves against, was placed in their midst through
evacuation was what can only be described as – 'Towneyism'.

The circumstances of evacuation organisation did not help. It occurred at the end of the school holidays, and therefore the maximum length of time had passed since school head inspections. It appears that those children who did not leave the towns with head lice, had them on arrival at their destination. Many travelled with an unfortunate mixture of food on trains with no loos and predictable results. Few had clothes or shoes appropriate to country living and no adequate allowances were made by the authorities to deal with this. The relationship between stress, anxiety and bedwetting was not commonly understood, and certainly evacuees were anxious and stressed. There were no clear allowances to be paid for capital equipment ruined and therefore the issue of bedwetting and ruined bedding became a significant one to rural housewives who had often acquired the material comforts of their cottages through intensive labour and parsimony. The greatest problem was however a cultural clash, fuelled by the rural women's confidence that their way of life was the embodiment of Englishness, which was after all what was being fought for. In the case of child evacuees on their own, the problem was in a sense soluble. It was possible for these children to adapt culturally, to a greater or lesser degree, to a rural way of life even if this was done at some emotional cost, whereas, when mothers were evacuated the result was usually disastrous. As one letter to *Home and Country* put it, 'We have learnt by actual contact how differently the other half of the world lives; we have seen too the other half appreciates us as little as we appreciate them'.[31] The writer went on to explain that she saw the policy of evacuating women from the towns as sexist. They should stay put as men did. Certainly many women could interpret the ideology of rural women as mothers of the nation and expand it out to see their work as of national importance; part of defeating Hitler. In *Diary of a Provincial Lady*, the stoical vicar's wife copes with large numbers of children running riot over the previously childless vicarage. The children block the drains, experimenting to see if fircones float in the toilet. She clings firmly to the idea that nothing matters but the total destruction of Hitler.[32] However, ideology is rarely absorbed so uncritically.

Stories and myths about the behaviour of town mothers, their personal hygiene (or lack of it) abounded. They have a distinct similiarity to the similarly unpleasant, racist myths that operate within post-war Britain. It could be argued that what is signified in these myths is a perception of the town inhabitants as less than human, less civilised, which in turn naturalises mistreatment and separation of them. Some stories, relating fundamentally to eating habits of children, were at one level humorous and signify their immaturity or lack of proper education and by implication their inadequate upbringing. For example, the five-and-half year old who asked for beer and cheese for supper or 'One little boy more used to the story of Goldilocks than a good hearty breakfast, who looked in horror at a plate of porridge and announced that he thought it was bear's food'.[33] Other stories are indicative of the different culture and morality required to survive in an urban rather than a rural environment. For example, 'One boy returned to his billet with a live hen under his arm and informed his landlady he could get plenty more for her'.[34] Myths and stories of town children with light fingers abound. In the fictionalised 'Jottings of Miss Toombs of Mudham' in *Home and Country* in 1940, Miss Toombs describes the embarrassment of discovering her evacuee Doreen has helped herself to a number of figurines from the mantlepiece of the local manor house, where the Christmas party was held. Although this particular column was tongue-in-cheek, what these myths or stories signify is the rural women's resentment that if they looked after evacuee children properly they were out of pocket. It must be remembered that wartime is in many ways associated with women being able to earn comparatively well in munitions, for example. Admittedly this was, in all probability, not the common experience of women war workers; however, in trying to understand issues around evacuation, perceptions and meanings are all important. The treatment of women who hosted evacuees can be seen as an extension of the poor status in which domestic labour was held culturally. One writer in *Home and Country*, taps into the financial hardship of those women whose war work was looking after evacuees rather than working in munitions factories and argues of housework:

> because it brings in no money, it also brings in very little understanding and respect, so little indeed that the planners of the evacuation scheme could – and did – calmly assume that the housewife need not be paid anything for the time, energy, labour and skill spent in cooking, washing, ironing, mending and 'minding' and doing housework for three or four extra children. They did not ask school buses to run free services with unpaid drivers; or farmers to charge nothing for milk and vegetables, or cobblers not to send in accounts for mending evacuated children's shoes. Housewives playing their part (mostly with affection and efficiency) nevertheless asked themselves – and the billeting officer –

the reason why they alone could be forced to work without pay. But answer came there none.[35]

This extract demonstrates a feminist response to the Government's treatment of rural women; based upon the perception developed by the Women's Institute Movement that they were skilled workers. Certainly evacuation was a very mixed experience for the host women, not to speak of the poor children and one of the few areas that they could verbalise and validate this was through the Women's Institute Movement. The NFWI collected responses of institutes to evacuation into a booklet published in 1940 *Town Children through Country Eyes'*.[36] Certainly, by putting it in print, this legitimated some of the worst of 'Towneyism', but it was in itself a contradictory document allowing for different readings. Stories of the children when negative were usually framed by a sense that these children had been redeemed by country life, they had grown, put on weight and learnt to eat proper meals for example. They had been successfully culturally assimilated.

What a myth signifies is a site of contestation, thus for some in the Movement the responses to evacuation and the glimpses it gave rural women of urban culture and living conditions fuelled the demands for social reforms, and the need to build a new Britain after the war. In writing about the evacuation survey in *Home and Country* for example, Esther Neville Smith, on behalf of the NFWI subcommittee, says of the meaning of evacuation to the NFWI member:

> It stands for a glimpse into other peoples lives, and the resulting shock of finding so many of these lives were to her hardly imaginable. Many country dwellers are used to a lack of modern amenities, but what was revealed was something beyond discomfort: it was a state of living which put out of the reach of numberless families that quality of home life to which every one has a claim.[37]

This statement contains the dubious assumption that what constitutes a quality of home life is not open to question in class and gender terms. What can be read from such a statement is that evacuation convinced many members that society was failing significant numbers of the population. I mentioned, in relation to the World War One, theories that in order to gain consensual support for war the Government needed to offer the population more in the post-war period, than the maintenance of the status quo. Similarly in the 1939–45 War, a better society needed to be fought for. The experience of evacuation may have served to fuel some of the demands for post-war social welfare reform. It is this area, the attempt to plan for the building of a new Jerusalem in the post-war era to which I now want to turn.

Addison has described the building of a consensus which led to the post-war settlement, citing the significance of: Labour party members of the Cabinet, the extension of planning, and Government intervention in the economic, social and welfare issues within the nation.[38] Furthermore, the Army Education Corps has always been given much credit for spreading ideas of socialism and for helping to build a consensus in support of the Beveridge Report, the Welfare State and the 1945 Labour Government. Yet organisations like the NFWI were also very significant in helping to create the consensus which supported a much greater role for Government in the post-war era. Although the NFWI was emphatically non-party political and contained members of all political parties, the social reforms it advocated, in order to improve the material circumstances of rural women's lives, stood almost no chance of implementation by other than a left-wing government and some, such as equal pay for men and women, not even by them. I have already explored how during the 1920s and 1930s the NFWI had increased its demands for rural water supplies, drainage, electricity and well designed and reasonably priced rural housing for the working class. These demands in the wartime were seen as the basis of any post-war reconstruction.

By 1940 *Home and Country* announced that post-war planning conferences were being held up and down the country, and that twenty-eight counties had already made bookings for speakers from headquarters. In her speech to the AGM in 1943 Lady Denman reminded the Federation of its role in pressure group politics in the framing of policy for post-war planning.[39] The role of institutes in gathering information from members on education and housewives' requirements in the post-war home were seen as significant as was the role of NFWI representatives on Government committees. Despite the misguided notion of one rather naïve member in the 1920s, who suggested raising the funds for water supplies in the villages by rummage sales, in the main the Government at a local and national level was perceived as supplying these reforms. What changed during the war was the movement's perception of the Government's ability and power to act. In 1940 one astounded member wrote to *Home and Country* about how, in the pre-war period, her village had campaigned unsuccessfully for rural water supplies, only to discover when the army were stationed near by their camp had water and drainage in no time at all. Why, this member wanted to know, couldn't such action be taken for ordinary people in peacetime?[40] In the pre-war period the campaigns had perhaps been perceived to be about the more even or equitable distribution of scarce and limited Government funding. In the operation of World War Two that very notion of Government finance being severely limited was undermined. Furthermore, from evacuation to rationing and the regulation of female labour, the ordinary WI member, during the war, had begun to have a different perception of the Government's role in everyday life. This helped to naturalise the idea of a managed economy. This was all to become part of the movement's re-negotiation of their perception of Englishness and the England that they were fighting for. It was a perception that contained both continuity and change. Indeed these themes (as I have previously argued in chapter three) were given space in a NFWI publication about themselves in 1943 which reworked the association of ruralism and heritage to include state-provided housing, water and sewage. In other words, an improved and modernised infrastructure, not just a romanticisation of the past, was to be part of British heritage.

At times, the nature of the reconstructed Britain that the movement wanted is somewhat elusive and rhetorical. One letter to *Home and Country* claimed that, 'The WI movement will be able to do a tremendous lot in the sort of reconstruction that in the end will be so much more important than building new houses'.[41] The numerous homeless may not have shared this sense of priorities. At a West Sussex conference on wartime programmes it was argued, 'The need of the future should also be taken into account and the foundation laid for an England more approaching Blake's ideal'.[42] Given that Blake's 'Jerusalem' has been used as an anthem by both the Labour and Conservative parties in the post-war era, it is obviously no simple matter to define a version of Jerusalem. It was open to a variety of interpretations and maybe that is part of the essence of the popularity of post-war reconstruction epitomised by what I would regard as almost the ultimate polysemic text – the Beveridge Report. Like the Army Education Corps, the NFWI studied the Beveridge Report earnestly. Articles were written about it in *Home and Country*, day schools and conferences held on it at county level. Local institutes had discussions and wrote letters airing their views which were varied, though in essence supportive. Many saw the Beveridge Report as at last recognising the importance of the housewife's role as a skilled worker. Helen Judd writing in *Home and Country* proclaimed, 'Housewives have come into their own at last ! The Beveridge Plan for social security ... puts in its own words "a premium on marriage instead of penalising it".'[43] Family allowances, widow's benefits, maternity grants and health care are seen as positive and part of the recognition of women's domestic labour to the nation as a whole. In 1943 a proposed resolution for the AGM states that, 'This meeting records its appreciation of Sir William Beveridge's great work for social security and particularly of his recognition that health insurance for housewives and family allowances are essential if family life is to be free from want'.[44] It was passed unanimously. However the Government's proposals for a social insurance scheme in 1944 did not meet with the same level of approval. Cicely McCall (who resigned from her job at the NFWI headquarters in 1945 to stand unsuccessfully as a Labour candidate) challenged members to examine the proposed scheme and bring up points of disagreement for the next year's AGM. Members were asked to consider a number of questions such as whether housewives should be excluded from paying national insurance contributions and from sickness benefits, whether the payment of twenty pounds for a death and only four pounds for a birth was equitable, whether men and women should have different retirement ages and whether maternity payments should be higher for women who worked outside the home than for housewives?[45] Her chivvying of the membership obviously struck a chord and in 1945 the AGM passed a resolution requesting cash sickness benefit for all housewives and widows, not technically speaking gainfully employed.[46] In this, as with many other demands the NFWI made, they were to be disappointed.

As I have already said, the Women's Institute Movement was a diverse federal structure. Whereas an institute in one area might be avidly discussing post-war reconstruction, another would be totally pre-occupied with sewing-bees and digging for victory. By 1945 some institutes were certainly more political than others and a letter to *Home and Country* in 1945 by a woman of twenty seven, who was resigning from her local WI, indicates the problems that the movement was already experiencing as a result of having, perhaps, an older membership during the war. She claims:

> The whole policy of the WI certainly appeals more to the woman of say 45-50 who has no very definite political view, and who is more vitally

interested in say the weekly whist drive and cooking and needlework than the prefabricated house and the rehabilitation of servicemen and women and various other non-party subjects. When one realises the potential voting strength of women in so far as their own and their children's lives are concerned, I feel that the WI is throwing away a great opportunity of being a power for good in the fight for the equality of women.[47]

The writer feels that the NFWI will fail consequently to attract women returning from the forces. Her remarks were not unanimously well-received and indicate the diversity of the movement. Some felt that too much politics and feminism in the organisation was alienating the ordinary village women, whilst others stress the importance and popularity of political issues in the movement and another member made it quite clear that she did not want young members in her institute as they had nothing in common. There had been debate about the movement's role in wartime and this continued in the post-war period. Certainly during the war the NFWI continued to espouse its own brand of feminism. They continued to give women space to challenge the dominant value system's perception of housework. They saw themselves as skilled workers and were prepared to speak out when they saw themselves being exploited as with the evacuation experience. The NFWI women saw their post-war Jerusalem in terms of a re-negotiation of domesticity, its status and the power relationships around it. They saw the liberating potential of an equal but different role for women. Social welfare legislation and post-war reconstruction with, for example, the introduction of the NHS, promises of Government house building and maternity grants offered the hope that this might be achieved. To achieve this end they were happy to use and re-negotiate the concept of Englishness. With the benefit of hindsight it may seem that their ideas were naive and liable to be incorporated by the right. I do not, however, think they should be rejected. They may hold the key to building a truly widespread feminist movement, especially when the social welfare system of the post-war world is being dismantled at the expense, particularly, of women. In many respects the NFWI were to be disillusioned and disappointed and I will explore how they reacted to this in the final chapter. Now I want to explore part of the NFWI's own post-war reconstruction project – Denman College.

NOTES

1. C. McCall, *Women's Institutes*, London 1943, p31.
2. *Home and Country*, May 1940, p95.
3. Explored in more detail in Angus Calder, *The People's War* Panther, London 1969.
4. *Home and Coutry*, June 1940, p111.
5. See further, T. Harrison, *Living Through the Blitz*, Colins, London 1976.
6. *Home and Country*, October 1939, p312.
7. *Home and Country*, May 1942, p91.
8. E.M. Delafield, *The Diary of a Provincial Lady*, London 1947, reprinted Virago, London 1984, p388–89.
9. *Home and Country*, September 1940, p157.
10. *Home and Country*, January 1941, p17.
11. B. McBryde, *A Nurse's War*, London 1986, p112.
12. *Home and Country*, January 1942, p6.
13. *ibid.*
14. This and much of the following detail relies on the Produce Guild file in the NFWI archive.
15. *Home and Country*, January 1941, p3.
16. *Home and Country*, February 1941, p48.
17. *Home and Country*, June 1944, p12.
18. Langton Maltravers WI War History, in the History File in NFWI archive.
19. Mrs Anchor, oral Interview (1).
20. *ibid.*
21. N. Last, in R. Brood and S. Flemming (eds.), *Nella Last's Diaries*, Falling Wall Press, Bristol 1981.
22. *Keeping Ourselves Informed*, NFWI publication, London 1981, p38.
23. Mrs Anchor, *op cit.*
24. *Home and Country*, June 1942, p114.
25. P. Wright, *On Living in an Old Country*, Verso, London 1985, p24.
26. Many of the following details come from the Wartime file in the NFWI archive.
27. E.M. Delafield, *The Diary of a Provincial Lady*, London 1947, reprinted Virago, London 1984, p384.
28. E.M. Delafield, in *Home and Country*, March 1939, p99.
29. E.M. Delafield, *The Diary of a Provincial Lady*, London 1947, reprinted Virago, London 1984, p385.
30. *Home and Country*, August 1939, p261.
31. *Home and Country*, December 1939, p367.
32. E.M. Delafield, *Diary of a Provincial Lady*, London 1947, reprinted Virago, London 1984, p389.
33. 'Town Children through Country Eyes', NFWI publication, Dorking 1940, p7.
34. *ibid.*, p13.
35. *Home and Country*, June 1942, p114.

36. 'Town Children through Country Eyes', NFWI publication, Dorking 1940.
37. *Home and Country*, April 1940, p87.
38. P. Addison, *The Road to 1945 – British Politics and the Second World War*, London 1975.
39. *Home and Country*, July 1940, p112.
40. *Home and Country*, May 1945, p13.
41. *Home and Country*, December 1941, p251.
42. The West Sussex Supplement to *Home and Country*, December 1941.
43. *Home and Country*, February 1943, p36.
44. *Home and Country*, July 1943, p112.
45. *Home and Country*, August 1944, p161.
46. *Keeping Ourselves Informed*, NFWI publication, London 1981, p148.
47. *Home and Country*, January 1945, p23.

7

DENMAN COLLEGE

During World War Two the NFWI, like many other organisations and groups of the period, had been involved in thinking about and discussing post-war planning. They had been determined that Britain after the war would not be a continuation of the 1930s complete with unemployment, poverty and inequality. Improving the lot of rural women was as always their foremost concern and they expected the movement to change and be innovative. Denman College, a residential adult education college for WI members which opened in 1948 was perhaps the most lasting and significant example of this. Denman College became central to the NFWI's perception of itself, its version of Englishness and practical feminism, offering as it did a female-controlled and oriented holiday. It was hoped that for the women who would attend the college it could provide a space to acquire new skills, have a rest, and experience the confidence and consciousness-raising effects of an all female environment. Some saw it as offering opportunities for women through education. It could be argued that the emphasis on education was an attempt at a version of egalitarianism which was about broadening access to middle-class culture rather than supporting or providing a space for the development of working-class women's culture as the local institutes had often done. Like other areas of the organisation, Denman's role, its meaning to members and leaders of the Women's Institute Movement, was by no means straightforward but rather open to contestation, struggle and renegotiation. In this chapter I am therefore going to concentrate on the following areas: the founding and organisation of Denman College, the perceptions of those involved in this, the experience of attending the college for the members, and the role the college came to play in the movement.

The idea of a NFWI residential college was first mooted in 1943 at a four day residential course held by the movement in Shrewsbury on 'Education and the Planning of the Future Welfare State'. Sir Richard

Livingstone, President of Corpus Christi College, Oxford and an expert on adult education, prompted by Adeline Vernon and Cecily McCall of the NFWI, suggested the college. Pointing to the Government 's lack of proposals for adult education he suggested the NFWI should found a people's college. Cecily McCall reported the occasion in *Home and Country thus*:

> The high spot of the conference was the idea Sir Richard left with us. A conference house where we could meet together for a day or longer ... a hostel, holiday home (with nursery attached) ... .Just an outsize dream, not if we want it enough. Then it might just become a thrilling possibility.[1]

Progress was slow, but the idea gained some currency throughout the movement although some of the NFWI executive were not unduly enthusiastic. In 1944 NFWI headquarters produced notes on 'The Proposal for a Women's Institute College'. The perceived purposes of the college were described thus, 'A Countywoman's College would provide an opportunity for the education and personal development of rural women and girls (WI members only) and would act as a source of motive power in rural reconstruction'.[2] The notes go on to point out the increasing numbers of members were demanding further facilities for studying questions of the day and cultural subjects. They point out the very positive experiences of residential schools, which provide a period of study undisturbed by home pre-occupations during which they can associate with some distinguished men or women and with fellow members who have a similar interest but a different background'.[3] They also felt, 'The facilities would be especially valuable to younger women from the forces who could be shown the possibilities of rural life'.[4] In line with the spirit of post-war planning they also saw the college as potentially opening up the movement in democratic terms, claiming that:

> The college would also give her (the ordinary WI member who had possibly left school at 14) a special opportunity for seeing the scope and power of the WIs and discussing their future direction and character; it ought to encourage more members to stand for County and National Federation committees and would lead to greater democracy throughout the NFWI.[5]

There is in this the sense that education and political awareness are somehow intrinsically linked, a notion that both the political left and the post-suffrage women's movement seemed to share in the first half of the twentieth century. Such thinking perhaps relies upon a rather narrow definition of what political awareness is, and sees politics principally in relation to the electoral system. Embedded within this quote, also, are some of the ideals of the 1945 Labour government, which lay behind the founding of the Arts Council, the scholarship system of entry to Grammar school and the post-war expansion of higher education, the belief that greater opportunities and access to cultural and academic education needed to be offered to the nation as a whole to bring about a redistribution of power. What such premises ignore is the internalisation of subservience, which allows the naturalisation of class, race and gender power relationships. However egalitarian their motives, few of the NFWI leadership were able to interrogate the operation at both the practical and ideological levels of class hegemony within which Denman College operated. With the benefit of hindsight, the intentions can be seen as worthy and radical whilst their limited effectiveness is acknowledged.

At the 1945 AGM Oxfordshire County Federation's resolution in favour of the proposed college was debated. It read:

> That this meeting welcomes the suggestion of a Women's Institute college, notes with satisfaction the power to provide grants for such a purpose in Clause 100 of the Education Act 1944 and instructs the executive committee to make the necessary arrangements.[6]

There was not unanimous support for the resolution. Indeed, it was passed by only twenty votes (each of over 5000 institutes having one vote) with South Stokes's amendment instructing the Executive Committee to make necessary arrangements. A delegate to the AGM summed up some of the objections to the college for her report in *Home and Country*:

> – a Warwickshire member drew a storm of clapping when she pointed out that the ties of home and children meant that students would be drawn chiefly from one class of member. Shropshire also against the resolution, thought it unfair to ask the ordinary member to raise money for something which would only benefit the few, and when a member from an East Kent WI showed that only 3,000 of our 300,000 members could attend a year it looked as if the resolution would be lost.[7]

In time all these fears were to be realised, however the college's role was symbolic for many members. It was to be a potential opportunity the NFWI offered even if it was realised by very few and predominantly the middle-aged and middle class. Thus in terms of class this could be said to reflect post-war education policy nationally.

Following the AGM, attempts began to find a house and to finance the purchase. The original hope of some Government financing was to prove disappointing but the Carnegie Trust offered twenty thousand pounds providing the NFWI could raise an equal amount. The initial method of raising funds was by each individual institute being asked to raise ten pounds over the next three years. In 1950 out of seven and a half thousand institutes over two thousand had still made no donation. It is interesting to speculate how many of these were from areas too far away from Denman to make frequent use of it. Certainly the high number of non-contributors indicates less than total support for the college. While the fundraising and the search for a suitable property continued, the name for the college was fixed as a tribute to Lady Denman, following her resignation as NFWI Chairman at the 1946 AGM. In 1947 the purchase of Marcham House, not far from Oxford, was arranged; Marcham having been the country house of the Duffield family until 1938. The property had been requisitioned by the RAF during the war and some refurbishment was therefore necessary. It was estimated that approximately twenty thousand pounds would be required to purchase and equip the college. The rest of the money raised went into an endowment fund to help cover the cost of upkeep of the property. When the college first opened it could only accommodate thirty students as the NFWI was initially unable to obtain the necessary building licence to convert the stables into bedrooms. Building licences and the conversion followed in 1949 with a further extension of bedrooms in 1953, which then enabled over fifty students to stay at Denman at one time. Many of the soft furnishings were provided by local WIs with County Federations adopting a room or part of a room as their responsibility. This then provided for those County Federations a practical and also an ideological sense of identification with the college.[8] Government finance turned out, in the long run, not to be hopeless and in 1948 the Department of Education made the first of what became annual grants to the NFWI for the 'liberal education of women' and allowed part of that grant to be allocated to Denman College.[9]

With the aim of opening the college by September 1948 the selection of a warden was considered. Betty Christmas who was chosen for this job, was heard to describe herself as the 'little girl from the country who made good'.[10] She had joined her local WI at Bures, West Suffolk, at only sixteen. She soon was active in local drama and became assistant secretary of her institute. She then progressed to working for the accounts department at NFWI. Following two years in South Africa she became County Secretary of the Buckingham Federation in 1935. In 1940 she returned to headquarters to become General Organiser. She was therefore very much a product of the movement. This biography of her comes from the official Denman history[11] in which she is the embodiment of a new post-war redefinition of 'the people' having reached her position as a result of hard work and merit, rather than by being a member of a titled family, this aligning her with a perception of the initial post-war period as one in which an ideal of the respectable and hard working middle class became central to definitions of the nation. Two further ex-county secretaries were appointed to the college staff and an ex-matron of Radbrook College.

The NFWI membership perceived Denman as an extension of the institutes in the villages. It was embedded in their minds with the same notions of Englishness and this had of course lain behind the choice of an eighteenth-century country house. It owed more to an élite perception of Englishness than the radical reworking Cecily McCall's book on the movement had offered. In time the image of Denman was to become an emblem of the movement and this created its own problems. Much assistance in the preparation of the college, the showing round of individual visitors, or visiting institutes was done by members of the National Federation executive and local institutes. In the 1940s when many local Institutes were working hard to assimilate Denman into their sense of identity, the employment of a German receptionist to show visitors around jarred. It was for them too soon after the war, in which Germany was seen as embodying all that was non-English – Other. Potters Bar and Little Heath WI wrote to protest in 1946:

> Sixty-four of our members visited Denman College on August 16 1948 where we were received by a German receptionist. All of those members were very disturbed by this and wish to protest to who ever is responsible for this appointment … .and request that action be taken to rectify this. We do not object to a job being given to any nationality but not as a receptionist to show members their own college. This does indeed seem wrong and will we feel have a adverse effect on the future of

Denman College.[12]

The Warden's reply pointed out that much work was done at Denman unpaid by local institutes and that Miss Goldschmitt should not 'be punished for an accident of birth' as she had been an institute member for over six years. What the incident does indicate, is how delicate the reworking of institutes and national identities were at that time.

The college was finally opened for the first students in September 1948 by Sir Richard Livingstone. During his speech he said that:

> It was the business of education to help people to learn things they wanted to do but could not do without help ... read books, enjoy music art, grow flowers and vegetables decorate a house, do needlework, bring up children, understand engines and the stars and much else. It is to teach people not when they are unwilling as they are in their school days, but when they are desirous and thirsty to learn. It is to tap the huge source of energy there is in human beings.[13]

Of course, all these things the Women's Institute Movement had already done for rural women. He went on to say, 'But one can't do this sort of thing at home. One needs a place to get away from household duties and worries and give one's whole time to the business at hand'.[14] The speech infers the emphasis of the movement's educational work once Denman College was in operation. The notion that somehow the really serious learning was done at Denman, rather than in the villages, seemed to grow. It appears that in the post-war period NFWI expertise was gained at Denman rather than in county or federation classes. This was a step in a somewhat élitist direction, as in reality so few members could go to Denman. Certainly, almost all the NFWI officer training or judge and demonstrator training was held, henceforth, at Denman instead of being held regionally around the country. This may have led to a more centralised southern bias. Furthermore, the cost to attend Denman was fifteen shillings a night for full board plus five shillings tuition fee, although as a significant number of students had their fees paid by their local authority, institute or other NFWI sources the fees were not as prohibitive as it might seem. These charges were well below the economic price and indeed financial problems, as a result of the wish to keep the cost of courses low, were a constant difficulty. Financial ideas such as the attempt to run an economically sound market garden and keeping hens were not a resounding success. Instead donations, appeals to the institutes and selling off parcels of land, or buildings from the estate were more sound providers of financial safety-nets for the college.

Courses at Denman were of two types – 'A' courses open to any member and 'B' courses which had restricted entry and were usually some kind of training for NFWI officers. There was, at first, something of an emphasis on 'B' courses as they provided a guarantee of willing students, however 'A' courses soon proved to be very popular.[15] The college, obviously, became the focus for much of the in-service training required of NFWI officers, for example 'Produce Guild Leader's School', 'Voluntary County Organisers' Training School' and 'Judges' and 'Demonstrators' schools. WI market organisers and many others flocked to Denman to be trained on 'B' courses. These courses were not open to ordinary members but were restricted to those recommended by their county federations and who had some already proven skill or ability in the subject area of the course. There was consequently limited scope for innovation in the subject of these courses. The 'A' courses put on by the college were varied and fairly consistent with areas studied by the movement in the pre-war era. The programme for 1950 included 'Pig Keeping and Curing', 'Soft Toy Making' and 'Smocking', 'Gardening' and 'Fruit Preservation'. There were also in 1949 four 'Country Housewives Courses', two of which were oriented towards Christmas. On the more academic side there were courses on 'Books and Music', 'The Victorian Age' and 'Feeding a Hungry World'. As the official history of Denman points out that in 1953:

> The popular courses such as 'Flower Arrangement', 'Patchwork', 'Dress Making' and 'Home Decoration' were usually over subscribed but some others were proving hard to fill. The least successful one had been on local government and social problems.[16]

Many of the most popular courses were of a practical nature and cookery courses followed the conversion, in 1952, of RAF huts into a demonstration kitchen and lecture room, a project undertaken in conjunction with Berkshire County Council.

Indications of the reasons for hesitancy concerning non-practical courses were given by one student interviewed in 1956. The following quote illuminates how attendance at Denman must be considered within the social context of the everyday lives of rural women in the NFWI:

I think there is a tendency to be nervous of what seem in print to be rather academic courses. And another thing when we come here we have to do rather a lot of arranging, leaving the children with kind friends and relatives persuading our husbands that the venture is going to benefit everyone. So when we go back, we like to show some newly acquired skill, whether it's icing cakes, painting pictures, taking photographs or knitting complicated jerseys. If we come to a course on music or history or something, well we don't seem to have anything to show for it![17]

The student who felt the pressure to learn something practical illuminates the somewhat ambiguous nature of women's leisure. Even in their week away from home, or perhaps particularly at such a time, rural housewives felt they must be servicing others. For housewives the leisure/work divide is never really complete; indeed, Denman College attendance can become a site for struggle over the meaning of activities for women. What is seen by the members as a site of leisure may be seen as an educational experience by husbands, family or the NFWI leadership. Alternatively, an activity like a visit to Denman may be represented as educational by rural women themselves in order to justify their visit.

The quote above comes from an article by Honor Watts in *Home and Country* in 1956, which unquestionably supports the more practical courses. These she feels entail the real 'work and skill'. But she also quotes a student who had attended a poetry course, as the patchwork course was full, and was able to enthuse the whole family about poetry, her contribution to the rest of the family's welfare thereby justifying what otherwise might be perceived as frivolous or selfish. The tone of the article is epitomised in the following extract of a student's comment to Honor Watts and her response. 'You've been highbrow today haven't you with local government. So clever of you'. How could anyone with the gift of cutting and stitching think it clever to sit and listen to a series of stories?[18] It is hard to comprehend what level of support Honor Watts had for her emphasis on practical subjects, or her derisory description of information on local government as 'stories'. The use of the word story is usually a signifier of low status, of something engaged in for pleasure – that is a leisure activity. Her words may be interpreted as consistent with an interpretation which elevates women's skills while seeing many male spheres as ideologically overrated. The radical implications of this contestation of the dominant cultural definitions of work and leisure should not be ignored. Despite this there were a steady stream of arts courses including ones in the Welsh language.

The early courses ran during the week, as it was thought easiest for students to get away during the week and it was difficult to obtain domestic staff to run the college at the weekends. Courses ran either until the Thursday or Friday morning and students had sessions most nights after supper as well as mornings and afternoons. Students usually arrived for supper on the Monday night, often having the first talk after that meal. This would frequently be either an introduction and history of Denman College, or if they were on a B course a more specialised subject. The history of Denman College as a building (which also occurs in the numerous souvenir histories produced for sale to students) emphasised, once again, Denman's links with a certain notion of the past, of Englishness and tradition. This is obviously a very selective version of the past. The growth in the acquisition of houses by the National Trust since World War Two indicates this selection of the past was not confined to NFWI members. The country house would have had different meanings to different social classes within the Women's Institute Movement and may well have alienated some. After all, if English country houses represented, to the bourgeoisie, culture, civilisation and quality, to the rural working class they usually represented a site of exploitation and badly paid long hours of toil.

Young women did not predominate and indeed it was thought necessary to ask institutes to let the college know if the member due to attend Denman was under twenty-five so that an effort could be made to find another younger member to stay at the same time. However, in 1957 a special drama course was put on for the under twenty-fives. Little was done to vary the range of members attracted to the courses. Despite deliberations which pointed out the advantages of weekend courses for women who worked, only one was included in the following year's programme in 1949. For the ordinary member it was not easy to leave home and family; the planned nursery, mentioned first in 1943, had never materialised; although the suggestion had been voiced again in 1947 the minutes of the Denman College sub-committee report that 'It was noted for further consideration but it was felt that there were various difficulties about the project'.

There is every indication that not all students found it easy to mix. When they came to the college for the first time, it could be an intimidating experience. Occasionally students of two or three courses would get together for a social evening. Courses usually incorporated a relevant outing. The 1950 'Pig and Bacon Curing School', for example, included a visit to a local pig farm. Occasionally there was a free afternoon in the course, but student questionnaires indicated no great enthusiasm for this; finding the two hour break between tea and supper sufficient for their needs.[19] It was found useful to have each course looked after by a chairman, (sic) who was usually a national, education or Denman College committee member. According to the notes for chairmen, they were perceived to have three main tasks:

(1) To act as hostesses and introduce speakers, and to stimulate discussion of their talks or demonstrations.

(2) To provide a thread of continuity between the different talks, excursions, demonstrations, film shows etc. and to link these up with opportunities in their own counties.

(3) To relate the content of the course to institute work and past achievements and to point out that one institute can do nothing but 7,000 united through county and National Federation can do much.[20]

The notes also pointed out that, many of those attending have only limited knowledge of the NFWI, its organisation, and the work it has done and could do in service to the community and the countryside both locally and nationally. Thus within the structure of women-only courses at the college there was a determined attempt to raise the consciousness of women, in respect of their movement's political potential. Whatever the aims of the organisers of the courses, students would selectively consume their lectures and discussions. The leadership had a long way to go in their attempt to raise feminist consciousness amongst those who came on one course, judging by the comments provided as feedback. After the 'Produce Guild Leaders' School' in November 1955 one member said:

An extremely nice cross section of members I am not particularly keen on 'women *en masse*' but enjoyed the social part immensely I think a VCO course would be most stimulating but unfortunately have too many commitments in civil defence for this.[21]

To this member at least, the notion of a women-only course obviously held a somewhat limited appeal. The very notion of chairmen, acting as hostesses, and their expected role, perhaps owes a great deal to the country house origins of so many of those involved in the organisation of Denman. It may also have contributed to the alienation and trepidation ordinary members may have felt about attending the college, underlining how the ideology of Denman was that of opening up access to middle-class culture for the working class and how in reality egalitarianism is so much more complex. The evening sessions held jointly between courses in the early years were dropped in the 1950s. They had attempted to include some cultural input, music or poetry reading, for example, into even the most practical courses. The reticence of some of the students indicated, perhaps, that this form of middle-class cultural imperialism was not always appreciated.

At the time, course chairmen wrote reports on all those attending the college, and students were also asked to fill in a questionnaire on their stay and the course content when they left. A few have still survived and are evidence of the somewhat candid nature of some course chairmen when describing both students and speakers who, often employed from outside the movement, laid themselves open for close, critical scrutiny. In summing up one speaker's contribution, a chairwoman of a 'Produce Guild Leaders' School' wrote that, 'It would appear that all the outside speakers were not perfect and it would cause less destructive criticism if this session were at the beginning of the school before Miss Sims gave her talk on speaking'.[22] Or in November 1951, 'You will be relieved to hear that Mr Higgs' talk at the PG Leaders' school was a great success. The one criticism I have is that he paces the room like a caged lion and fiddles with things as he talks'.[23] The experience of attending Denman was as varied as were the students. The conscientious chairman of a 'Books and Music' course, in the early days of Denman, reported that the group included:

> a twenty year old who worked in the county library, a member who had missed her schooling through illness and was thrilled with what the WI was doing for her, a member who had been to America and been to Trinidad and wanted to talk about it, a reticent member with an Oxford degree who came into her own taking charge of the party visiting the Bodleian Library, a lady from High Wycombe and Bloomsbury wearing trousers, and finally a member who took no part in discussion but sang lustily and often wrongly.[24]

For the NFWI members who went to Denman it was usually a unique and very positive experience, although its meaning and significance was varied and depended on their particular circumstances. For women who were not married, Denman may have provided a safe environment to have a holiday, as NFWI-arranged holiday tours did at a later date. It was not until the 1970s and 1980s, after all, that women-run holidays became more generally available. Indeed, even in the 1980s some members saw this as a significant role for Denman. Many other women, for the first time, found themselves freed from household obligations and looked after in an all women environment. This might lead them often to explore the nature of their socially defined roles and see themselves in a different light. Many of them wrote to express their appreciation in poems about the college, which may provide an indication of some of the meanings of attendance to ordinary members. Here is an example found in the Denman archive.

'Song of the Country Housewife'
(tune of 'There's a Tavern in the Town')

There is a college down in Berks
Down in Berks,
And there the Housewife leaves her carks
Leaves her carks
And her cares at home midst laughter free,
And never, never thinks of he.

Fare thee well for I must leave thee,
Do not let this parting grieve thee,
But be sure to keep the children spick and span
And span.
I'll be back on Friday, see that well we dine,
Or may a housewives' curse be thine.

She's left him for a life of ease,
Life of Ease;
She sits with notebook on her knees,
On her knees,
And jots down thoughts great and small,
And never has to think at all.

Fare thee well, etc.

For three grand days she's free from queues,
Free from queues.
She gives no damn for roasts or stews,
Roasts or stews,
But tunes her brain to wavelengths clear of joints,
And never, never thinks of points.

Fare thee well, etc.[25]

This song, written in 1948, epitomises the spirit of the early days of Denman College and the Women's Institute members who attended. It celebrates freedom from caring for others, particularly husbands, described as 'he' in the first verse. Articles in contemporary magazines indicate that many women, who had been independent and self-sufficient during wartime, did not find the homecoming of the conquering hero all sweetness and light. One firewoman complained to Leonora Eyles of *Woman's Own* in 1945, 'I love the work and have put myself into it; although I long for the war to end all the suffering, I dread it because it means my going back to the emptiness of my life'.[26] Denman also represented for many women a unique break from housework, true female leisure. For three days they 'lived a life of ease' free from struggling with rationing, at this time more severe than even during the war. This element of staying at Denman ties in with schemes some institutes had in the 1930s to give a member from another institute a rest-holiday. The whole institute contributed to caring for the visitor, while her home institute helped care for her family. To many women a visit to Denman was the first holiday they had had in their married life and one woman remarked 'Oh, how wonderful to lift the lid of a dish and not know what's inside'.[27] There is every indication that to these women the reference in the song to thoughts 'great or small' that were being directed their way on courses about subjects as varied as 'Stage Management' or the 'Advanced School for Produce Judges' were perceived as qualitatively different from the thinking required for the management of a home. The home required stressful working thought, emphasising the continuous NFWI perception that housework was real work, undervalued by others but seen by the movement as important as the work of any man. After all, housework required thought and planning in the same way as the jobs of the predominantly middle-class, professional husbands of the women who came to Denman. Another poem from the Denman archives, probably written in the 1950s, also stresses the educational advantages of a visit to Denman.

'The Ode' by M.J. Saville

Members, living near the city,
Old or young, or plain, or pretty,
If you have a thirst for knowledge
Take a course at Denman College!
Any craft you care to learn
Is catered for, you need not yearn
For skill to handle this or that –
A four day course – you've got it pat.

The drawback to this plan I know,
Is what will happen, when you go
And leave your loved ones far behind?
Well wipe that thought clean from your mind
Twill give them all a chance to ponder
How absence makes the heart grow fonder
Don't let yourself imagine that
You'll find them stretched out on the mat,
Quite senseless from grief and hunger
(Whilst you've been feeling ten years younger!)

If hubby can't survive four days
Without your pretty winsome ways,
You've brought him very badly up.
Serve him no more from breck till sup!
Make him a list of all the things
The household chores, which each day brings,
Let him feed the dog, and cat,
Himself and chickens, what's that?
If he's unfit with these to wrestle –
Why call us the weaker vessel?[28]

Certainly, when women chose to go on a course at Denman, the freedom from housework was significant to them. Their visit did, as this poem suggests, also raise issues around women's right to leisure and the status given to women's skilled domestic labour, but the emphasis of this poem is on the women's desire for a skill or knowledge for her own gratification, not in order to better service her household. Thus the significance of Denman is seen as enabling women to create the space to do something just for themselves. The satisfaction of which was summed up by one member of Heynes WI in their thirtieth birthday souvenir booklet, 'First of all I must say that only those who have been, and those that will follow after, will know the privilege I have had in going to Denman College. Believe me it has been one of the greatest joys of my life and I mean just that'.[29]

In 'The Ode' there is also a sense that men have a problem coping with domestic labour, further proof of what women suspected all along – their incompetence. This is perhaps stressed more strongly in another poem which describes the return home thus:

> 'Twas on a Saturday morning
> When we beheld the dishes
> We came back to reality
> And rolled our sleeves up high.[30]

Such songs could be read as a grumble about male selfishness or a resigned acceptance of it, but I think this is too simplistic. Rather they fit in with what is all too familiar in female subcultural groups, well-worn stories of men's incompetence when women are ill, which can be understood as proof of women's skilled status as housewives. Thus they provide validation for rural housewives' role in the inability of men to substitute for them. Men's incompetence as housewives' substitutes can be seen as undermining, the social construction of masculinity as superior. Futhermore, Denman was also uniquely and significantly an all-women college and the importance of that underlies so much of its positive effect on the women who came there. This all female space probably also helped to bring about a good deal of the 'laughter free' in the 'Song of the Country Housewife'; such situations can also cause women to question why the laughter is not so free when men are about. A member on a 'Produce Guild Leaders School' in 1955 summed up the enjoyment in female fellowship when questioned about her magazine reading at the college said 'I devoted my spare time to conversations with my fellow students'.[31]

Some found the Denman courses over the years changed the pattern of their future lives. In 1973 the then warden of Denman College wrote about this:

> I do know of members who came on a writing course and have since had books published; of someone who felt stimulated to embark on a three year teacher's training course; of people who have dared to put brush to canvas for the first time and have found a life long hobby, of someone who has taken on the staging of large exhibitions after getting enthused at a college staging course ... of people who have found at the college just that release from nervous tension or paralysing isolation which has given them the courage to face life anew.[32]

Certainly for the majority of students Denman College, like so many of the movement's activities, from the monthly meeting to local WI classes and clubs, provided a space for women to fight the internalisation of their own oppression. They could gain self-confidence, and acquire new skills in an all women environment free from the critical scrutiny of the male gaze. The college was undeniably a positive experience for those who went. However as the college celebrated its fifth birthday, NFWI officers and officials were being trained at Denman but ordinary members were still clamouring just for a day-visit to see the college. Such visits were restricted to a two week period when the college was not being used for classes. In the years following the opening, waiting lists of those who wished to visit or attend a course grew and with it agitation and alienation. Even as late as 1953, according to the annual report, the warden claimed that all institutes which had been waiting for three years could be fitted in during the one week that year when the college staff would be stewarding.[33] A policy of accepting applicants first from institutes which had not previously had a member attend the college was aimed at ensuring the college attendance was as truly representative of the membership of the movement as possible. It did result in correspondence from discontented institutes complaining that the policy 'penalises WIs keen to support the college from its inception and those institutes with annual Bursaries'.[34] It was pointed out at the time, that despite the increased accommodation as a result of the stables conversion 'if every institute in the country had a Bursary then they would only be able to use it every fourth year'.[35] Denman was experienced only by very few of the movement. In 1953 only eight-and-a-half thousand members had attended Denman out of a total NFWI membership of approximately half a million. There is every indication that because of practical difficulties the college was not in class terms evenly utilised by the membership. A gardener in the early period remarked that there seemed a significant difference in class terms between those who visited the college and those who stayed.[36] With the existence of bursaries this cannot just be attributed to the cost of coming to Denman, although it is hard to speculate on who benefited most from the bursaries. Some local authorities also gave grants towards the cost of a course at Denman but this was almost exclusively for B courses and therefore not really available to the majority of members. It seems more likely that the country house ethos and aura of Denman may have intimidated and alienated certain sections of the membership, especially if they had not even paid a visit to Denman during a local Institute outing. Maybe the fears of some members before the college was built were being realised: it was not a college many members could visit.

It was, however, of growing symbolic importance to the movement. The image of Denman College with all the connotations of a tradition of English country house life was to become an emblem for the movement, almost a symbolic heart of the NFWI. In terms of the wider organisation this was a catastrophe; the version of tradition and Englishness so eloquently argued for by Cecily McCall in 1943, imbued with socialism, was gone. It was being replaced by a building with an élitist tradition run as a college attended by only a very tiny proportion of the membership. The heart of the movement had always been the village hall, occasionally the AGM or the Eccleston Street headquarters, a democratic ideal Denman did not compete with; it was controlled by a management committee and ultimately by the National Executive (without a long reputation of, or the background for, understanding the grassroots of the Women's Institute Movement). At Denman, courses which were predictably successful in number terms or which trained NFWI office holders predominated. This led to a conservative selection of courses in the villages a reticence to go in new directions in the educational side of the Movement. Members began to look towards Denman to provide their expertise and define desirable education for the NFWI.

As the popularity of the college grew, it provided more courses and so the staff had to be increased. Unfortunately the warden, Betty Christmas, became ill although she continued to work for two or three years until 1955 when, following the award of an OBE, she resigned.

The staff continued to operate the College as they had during her illness. Denman also suffered losses in terms of personnel from its regular speakers and the Denman committee. It was thus a time of uncertainty and change for the college. Although the absence of a warden for two years did not prevent the college running and it even began to branch out into some innovative courses, 'Science and the Ordinary People' being one of the more successful, followed up by 'Science the Housewives' Friend'. Other new courses were less well received; 'The Problems of Old Age' in 1956 was cancelled due to lack of support. By the end of 1956 once again the college was also in deficit and by even more than the previous year. It was felt necessary to put up fees. Finally the responsibility for college affairs was re-organised under a Denman College Committee to be responsible for domestic affairs, previously dealt with by the House Committee, and the courses, previously under the control of the Education subcommittee of the NFWI. Denman was then in a state of change and flux when it was suggested Cecily McCall should be appointed warden. Since her involvement in the instigation of the Denman ideal in the wartime era, she had been involved in a variety of other areas. After involvement in social work, she was, in the mid-1950s, working for the National Health Service in Norfolk. However, giving up her cottage and her pension rights, she arrived in August of 1957. Probably dismayed by the gap between the idea of the college and the actuality, Cecily McCall initiated a number of radical and feminist proposals. The history of the college describes it thus:

> She believed that the college had become inward looking, and that change was being resisted for the sake of keeping things as they always have been. Her first job as she saw it was to 'Let in the Light'. She wanted to widen the whole range of courses so that the college became a spearhead for the education of women.[37]

Within a month *Home and Country* carried the message that institute outings would be welcome at any time of the year not just in the two weeks when the college was closed in the summer.[38] Applications poured in, as after all some institutes had been waiting two or three years to visit. Although rife with practical problems, this idea was an important first step in closing the gap between Denman and the movement. Ordinary members would all at last get a chance to see the college, not just to fund it. To see it actually operational, it was hoped, would reduce the fear, distanciation and nervousness of ordinary members when it came to applying for courses. Indeed, in the period of January to July 1958 the warden was able to report:

> The college is open to visiting institutes five days a week and 210 parties have seen over the college since January the first. The effects on applications for courses is considerable and the members apply at once for future courses.... The total number of applications for six months for programme fifteen equalled the total number of acceptances for the whole twelve months of programme 14.[39]

Opening the college for visitors was not the only innovation, it was but one of a package to widen the attendance at Denman. With the building of a new dining room it was felt that day students could be accepted. This enabled NFWI members from surrounding institutes to visit the college when they otherwise might not have had the chance. This may have been a politically very astute move in view of the large amount of support from surrounding institutes that Denman had drawn on, since its inception, to show visitors around for example. Cecily McCall's determination to open the college to the membership was voiced in *Home and Country* in 1958 thus:

> Denman College belongs to the whole movement. Besides having an open door to the members who own it and want to visit their property, it must be accessible to all who want to attend courses whatever their family or work commitments. So this year the college will be open for all bank holidays and for 27 weekend courses. There will be a mothers and babies week this month and two weeks of family courses in August.[40]

The style of this article, called 'Denman College Tomorrow', is also different. Gone is the emphasis on the 'big cool hallway', 'the chandeliers' and the great skills and abilities of the students that Honor Watts put in her article on Denman in 1956[41] and early souvenir booklets. Instead Cecily McCall's article is accompanied by pictures of busy students not the imposing house. The only reference to the house points out its first occupants had eloped to Gretna Green. Thus she invoked the associations of romantic fiction, a traditional subcultural form of female leisure and escapism. Dismay is expressed that over half the institutes have never sent a member to Denman, which is portrayed as a place for enjoyment and pleasure.[42]

A significant radical innovation was the mother and babies week, which enabled mothers of under threes to come to Denman and attend any of the three courses on offer that week; while their children were looked after in a crêche staffed by Barnado's trained nannies and NFWI helpers. During the evening sessions, after the children were in bed, baby-sitters were provided. Eighteen babies attended with their mothers and even one grandmother, Dr Enid Brown, a retiring member of the NFWI executive. The mothers' responses were of total enthusiasm, Mrs Pamela Eccles of Wiltshire wrote:

> I feel the benefits of this week were threefold. First, the complete break in the routine of house chores, and relaxation from the endless watching the needs of young children. Second, to be able to take advantage of expert tuition. Third to be able to make friends and discuss so many subjects with members of about one's own age and interests. I strongly recommend to any members with young children to attend a course during mothers and babies week as it will prove a most happy experience.[43]

The idea was unique and even attracted the BBC who sent a camera team to record the event for television.[44] Cecily McCall's aim of putting Denman in the forefront of women's education was being realised. Families week also seems to have been successful, when husbands were permitted to accompany wives, and 25 children between the ages of 8 and 15 camped in the grounds. They were able to accompany their parents on some course outings but it was considered to be in the parents' best interests to keep them out of the house. The radicalism of these ideas in the 1950s seems remarkable, even if only a few members could take advantage of them. They were providing a rare opportunity to young mothers at a time when the NFWI was perhaps beginning to be in danger of gradually becoming an older women's movement. Day students, family weeks and mother and baby weeks were to remain part of the Denman programme for some time to come, however, the other innovation of 1958 was not repeated in a hurry. That was the Flower Arrangement Exhibition and Competition opened by Constance Spry and attended by NFWI members and the public alike. It certainly opened up the College. However it also severely strained resources on top of all the other innovations.[45] There was also a real attempt to broaden the content of the courses and although some such as 'The Farm Worker and his Family 1760–1958' and 'Planning a New Town' did not recruit enough to run, others such as 'Problems of Race' and 'TV for the Family' were a success. The 1959 programme was planned with many similar courses which included an astronomy course with Patrick Moore, a week's course on 'South Africa from Boer War to Apartheid' and a weekend course on 'The Daily Press: Who Controls it, Edits it and Writes for it'. There were to be three mother and baby weeks with a maximum of twelve babies each week. However, before that programme came to fruition Cecily McCall had been asked to leave the college.

There remains some mystery over the decision that Cecily McCall should be made to resign. Archives at Denman College contain minutes of the Denman College subcommittee but the notes covering the period have been removed. Barbara Kaye in her book *Live and Learn*, on the history of Denman College from a somewhat pro-NFWI stance, claims that there was a staff crisis precipitated by Cecily McCall[46]. Indeed, some of the staff who had been used to the old regime did resign or threaten to. However other staff, namely the tutor Miss Wirgman resigned when the warden was dismissed, although she was persuaded to stay on a few months. Furthermore the bursar who had threatened to leave because she apparently couldn't get on with the warden left six months later anyway. Certainly the May following the December when Cecily McCall departed found the college with no warden, no tutor and no bursar. Improving the financial position was also given as a reason for Cecily McCall's dismissal, however, most of her innovations made financial sense at least in the long term. She was planning to utilise the capital invested in the building more fully as it was not to be closed every weekend or for two weeks for visiting WIs every summer. Day students would bring extra revenue with little extra expenditure, and her attempts to bridge the gap between the college and the local village institutes could be seen as a long term investment, given that the Institutes would always be seen as a significant source of finance for Denman. It seems far more likely that the problems were ideological and political. Cecily McCall's notion of the NFWI and of Denman were from the wartime period when the NFWI was still imbued with truly radical potential, or rather, when the constant tension within the leadership of the organisation between an upper-class paternalism tinged with a conservative notion of tradition on the one hand, and feminist liberal, if not radical, ideology on the other, was still an open debate. By the late 1950s the paternalist traditionalists had the upper hand and they could not give Cecily McCall's Denman (given the symbolic role Denman had by them taken on in the movement) the support it needed. In the next few years Denman College took a much more traditional path and few within the movement can remember, now, such innovations as mother and baby weeks.

In summing up the significance of Denman College, it has to be understood that it fulfilled a number of different roles for the movement, for the leadership and for those who attended the courses. Initially it was an emblem of a particular version of an English past and the NFWI's relationship with that, but also it represented an ideal that the past privileges of the elite were now accessible for everyone in the movement, in theory if not in actuality. For the women who attended, like so many WI activities, Denman provided a unique space for women, where they could explore and develop their own capacities and confidence without male scrutiny and demands. It was a space in which women were prioritised instead of marginalised, as they were in many areas of rural life. Thus they could struggle against their internalisation of oppression and this could lead to them challenging the meanings and priorities of socially defined male and female roles. Issues raised by a visit to Denman, families' reactions to it and what it did for women at an individual level could, and frequently did, therefore, lead to a re-negotiation of women's domestic role. As such it had a potentially feminist role within the movement. It is necessary to return to the wider movement and explore the changes and concerns in the post-war years of which Cecily McCall's dismissal was a symptom.

NOTES

1. *Home and Country*, October 1943, p32.
2. Denman College File, in the NFWI archive.
3. *ibid*.
4. *ibid*.
5. *ibid*.
6. *Home and Country*, May 1945, p27.
7. *Home and Country*, July 1945, p32.
8. Much of the day to day information about courses and the running of the College has been gleaned from papers, leaflets and files in the Denman College archive cupboard.
9. Denman College File, in the NFWI archive.
10. B. Kaye, *Live and Learn the Story of Denman College*, Collins, London 1970, p41-42.
11. *ibid*.
12. Letter in the Denman College archive.
13. B. Kaye, *op cit.*, p48.

14. *ibid.*
15. Denman College archive.
16. B. Kaye, *op cit.*, p67-8.
17. *Home and Country*, October 1956, p317.
18. *ibid.*
19. Student questionnaires in the Denman File in the NFWI archive.
20. Notes for Chairmen in the Denman File in the NFWI archive.
21. Notes on Produce Leaders' Schools, in the Denman College File at the NFWI archive.
22. *ibid.*
23. *ibid.*
24. Chairmen's Reports, in the Denman File in the NFWI archive.
25. In unmarked folder in the Denman College archive.
26. J. Waller and M. Vaughan Rees, *Women in Wartime*, McDonald Optima, London 1987, p123.
27. B. Kaye, *op cit.*, p59.
28. In unmarked folder in the Denman College archive.
29. Heynes WI, 'The Prime of Our Lives – Thirtieth Birthday Booklet', 1969, Denman College archive.
30. In unmarked folder in Denman College archive.
31. Student questionaires, in Denman File in NFWI archive.
32. *Home and Country*, September 1973, p17.
33. Denman College annual reports, 1953, in Denman College archive.
34. In unmarked folder in Denman College archive.
35. *ibid.*
36. Miss Yarn, oral interview (8).
37. B. Kaye, *op cit*, p43.
38. *Home and Country*, September 1957, p283.
39. Denman College Report, January–July 1959, in Denman College archive.
40. *Home and Country*, May 1958, p140.
41. *Home and Country*, October 1956, p316.
42. *Home and Country*, May 1958, p140.
43. *Home and Country*, July 1958, p205.
44. *ibid.*
45. B. Kaye, *op cit.*, p84.
46. *ibid.* p85.

8

CAN FLOWER ARRANGING BE FEMINIST?

The post-war period was one of change for rural women. The welfare state brought the National Health Service and Family Allowances, post-war reconstruction provided modern homes, improved amenities and transport to the villages and the consumer revolution of the 1950s offered the housewife labour-saving devices. The Women's Institute Movement itself therefore had to develop to meet the changing needs of rural women in a period of time often seen as the heyday of domesticity. The 1950s saw a reduction in the overtly political side of the movement. In *Home and Country* in the inter-war period monthly reports on Parliament had highlighted government actions, white papers and parliamentary bills affecting women, but by the 1950s they were replaced with a focus on consumerism, fashion and hairstyles. The NFWI's major activities included the launching of the 'Keep Britain Tidy Campaign' and flower arranging, whilst a member described a WI meeting thus:

> Then the social half-hour, a sheet of newspaper and six pins handed to each of us to make a hat for ourselves. Sternly resisted temptation to make replica of the hat in front of me which had an object like a shaving brush on it and concocted a modest little bonnet. No prize for me but thoroughly enjoyed myself everyone so friendly and kind.[1]

It is not easy to see feminism in this. However such activities should not be dismissed, with the 'condescension of posterity'.[2] as trivial or reactionary. Over half a million women joined the seven thousand Women's Institutes in the Movement's most popular period – the 1950s. By looking at the Women's Institute's version of women's politics, domesticity, femininity and Englishness I shall argue that for women at the end of the war a more limited, less overtly political, although still significant feminism emerged, intrinsically linked to improving the conditions of women's lives and re-evaluating domesticity.

World War Two had temporarily opened up a variety of new opportunities, in terms of work, for at least some women and in doing so it may have allowed for re-negotiation of the boundaries of femininity as changes which occurred in World War One did. *Behind the Lines*[3] points out, however, that the status differential between male and female spheres was not changed by war. If women were working in munitions factories and new heights of authority in the civil service, for example, this was significant but the really important high-status world had become the front, the theatre of war, from which women were excluded. Furthermore, during World War Two, the Home Front had been elevated to national significance. This had occurred in many spheres from the patriotic potato, the importance of canning and jam-making to the make-and-mend campaigns and dig for victory. This perhaps served to diminish the perceived gap in status between women's paid work and their unpaid domestic labour; although not between male and female spheres of paid or unpaid work. The appalling conditions, the long hours and the somewhat mundane, if not downright unpleasant, nature of much of women's war work may have been influential in the return of numerous women to domesticity at the end of the war. Many women may have been more than happy to settle for a 'semi' and two children in preference to ten or twelve hours a day in a munitions factory. For those women who had tried to combine motherhood and work during the war, domesticity may have offered the chance at last to do one job instead of two. Obviously personal circumstances differed and consequently there was much discussion and writing on domesticity in the post-war period.

If women for themselves were perceiving domesticity as having something to offer them, then the 1945 Labour government was fast convincing them that traditionally defined politics offered little. The marginalisation of women from the political process was increasingly achieved by Government measures such as the refusal to introduce equal pay (even in the Civil Service) and the refusal to introduce sick pay for housewives into the National Insurance scheme. Furthermore, women who were housewives and those with small children were further alienated from traditional politics by the introduction of double summertime, the stopping of the import of dried eggs to help the Balance of Payments crisis, the painfully slow improvement of rural water, electricity and sewage supplies, the introduction of bread rationing, the slow removal of rationing on tea, indeed, the whole issue of rationing itself. The letters pages of *Home and Country*, in the initial post-war period, were full of women's discontent and disenchantment about all these issues. In the male sphere of traditional politics women may have had the vote, but they seemed to have no voice, but by writing to the WI magazine they made their discontent public. They moved their grievance from the personal to the public sphere. Their position on rationing was not however straightforward; in 1946 the NFWI were willing to help with the distribution of ration books in areas where no suitable paid employees could be found, but they refused to discuss the issue of the introduction of bread rationing on the basis that it was a party political matter.[4] They lobbied Parliament about the particularities of rationing in relation to rural housewives, requesting more sugar for fruit preservation and pointing out the necessity of wellington boots for those living in rural areas. Rationing, however, remained in place until the 1950s to many housewives' dismay, as it seriously added to their domestic labour. In 1948 Ada Harrison wrote in *Home and Country* of her attendance at the NFWI Produce Guild Show[5] where she had heard the President of the International Federation of Agricultural Producers open the show. She explained to readers:

> Mr Turner is saying that there is in this country a widespread illusion that food will at some point come back with a rush but that is an illusion. I am conscious I entertained it.[6]

The desire of women post-war to purchase and consume goods without restrictions is indicated in this quote. However, *Home and Country* did carry numerous articles which kept up the wartime 'make and mend' impetus. In 1945 Lady Denman's AGM address demanded members 'Save, Sacrifice and Strive'.[7] Certainly instructions for garments to be made from parachute silk abounded. In June 1947 a rather moralistic short story warns the reader of coveting a green gown rather than being happy to wear an old dress or utility clothing. This story was also open to a reading which validated the desire for personal consumption and is a foretaste of the feminism of the 1950s and consumption's more potentially subversive role, which I shall look at later.

In the late 1940s the NFWI was constantly chivvying the Government to implement both small and large scale reforms, for example: to make analgesics in childbirth more widely available for rural women, to implement a scheme of relief milkers for agricultural workers and the greater provision of school meals. They joined with other women's organisations in demanding equal pay for women (particularly teachers who were in short supply) and in demanding that family allowances should be paid directly to mothers (not to fathers as originally suggested by the Government). They lobbied for rural water supplies not just when it was an economically viable proposition but as a right for rural women.[8] These issues straddle the perceived boundaries of equal rights and maternal feminism, and are not all specifically gendered issues, but they were all potentially able to improve rural women's lives. Furthermore there is evidence that the NFWI's perception of themselves as a powerful pressure group had some credence outside the movement. *The Times* in a 1951 article entitled the 'Growth of Women's Institutes' dubs them a force to be reckoned with concluding:

> The social consequences of the growth of the institutes are, in sum twofold. They have brought together women who in their own homes had mastered more than enough arts to qualify them as experts, but who had never learnt before to relax and to act as a corporate society. They have made audible for those outside the villages the voice of one hitherto inarticulate element in rural society.[9]

Although some of their campaigns were eventually successful, there was in the movement a sense of growing impatience at the inability of politicians to meet their demands. That the Government did not prioritise the concern of housewives seemed evident. Gradually the political issues that they adopted in the 1950s became of a less radical and more domestic nature. There were other reasons which also contributed to this.

The expansion of the welfare state and Government in the post-war period brought with it a mushrooming of both local and central Government experts. Official experts took over a variety of welfare issues which had previously been the sphere of expertise of women in the NFWI and similar organisations. The 1960s saw a re-invention of voluntary groups as experts, particularly as what has been described as the 'Poverty Lobby', but in the 1950s although the NFWI continued to give their opinions to a variety of Government bodies, they found themselves displaced by the centrality of professional experts. This contributed, in some sense, to the waning of the more overt NFWI political activities in the post-war period. There were, however, indications that the membership themselves were more inclined towards less political subjects and potentially in conflict with the leadership over this. The Chairman's address to the 1954 AGM indicates this:

> Does the Public Questions Handbook penetrate into general reading in the institutes?
>
> Are there a few perhaps rather earnest members who would like to see it, brushed aside in discussion by enthusiasts for basket making, cake icing and drama? Do we think public questions a rather dull sounding phrase?
>
> Yes it is dull to feel we have been concerned with bringing piped water to hard pressed countrywomen, who with aching backs and arms lugged buckets of water about until they feel old and battered before their time?
>
> ... isn't it rather splendid that we can feel personal pride at the sight of the trim and resolute policewoman to be seen in our market towns and villages, for we asked for them as long ago as 1922, 1934, and 1940. Are we not proud that countrywomen take such a large part in local government on county, district and rural councils, that they are constantly to be found actively engaged as school managers, and they are appointed as magistrates.
>
> In the Public Questions Handbook you will find the roots of so many things that flower in our midst.[10]

Despite this attempt to lay stress on the movement's political past and present pressure group power, the NFWI found itself floundering in political terms. The clear demands it had made, in previous decades, for any social welfare legislation that would improve the lives of rural women were replaced by AGM resolutions which tended to concentrate more on issues such as anti-litter campaigns, the removal of turnstiles in public loos, foot and mouth disease and uniform rental for telephones. Although of significance to rural women, they did not have the same level of gender-specific radicalism of earlier WI campaigns. They reflected, perhaps, the consensual politics which D. Dutton has described as the 'centrepiece of British political life'[11] at the time, whereby political differences could be seen in terms of the most efficient administration of a mixed economy rather than the degree of state intervention in the economy. Alternatively these issues (litter, turnstiles in loos) may be the ones on which the NFWI felt it could make some impact. This may be an example of the politics of the possible, rather than the ideological. For women's own perception of themselves this may be important. If the organisation was to help women feel empowered then it had to aim at what was achievable and to celebrate those of its demands which had been achieved, which the Women's Institute Movement does repeatedly. Social reforms which it had been demanding for many years were celebrated as they were introduced, whilst the Government was lobbied about the need for greater speed in implementing them. The survey carried out by the NFWI, with results published in 1957 as a pamphlet entitled 'Our Villages',[12] may be seen in this light. This recorded the movement's views on village amenities such as village halls, playgrounds, piped water and sewage, as well as what improvements were still needed. The NFWI Chairman, at the AGM, instructed members to buy a copy of the survey, compare their village to others and use it to pester parish councils. The improvement of rural life was, in her speech, still a significant concern:

> And we must do some stirring, we who seek to improve and develop conditions of country life must not quietly tolerate conditions that tend to drive people away from the country into town life with its equal but obvious advantages.[13]

Despite this emphasis by the Chairman, throughout the 1950s the social side of the movement was foregrounded and seen as making rural life more tolerable. The provision of a woman-only social centre in the villages had, perhaps always, been of primary importance to the members but in the 1950s the leadership, also stressed the social side of the movement. In 1957 *Home and Country* carried a series entitled 'Letters to a Very New Member' written by Jean Marwick. In one she writes, 'I do hope you have found the interest which the WI brings. The opportunities it offers and above all the friendship and the companionship without which most of us could not be'.[14] This same rhetoric is used in the Chairman's address at the AGM:

> You may have begun by feeling you didn't know a soul here, but WI fellowship breaks through that and we'll find new friends and good neighbours today all willing to help and be helped ... WI membership is the finest insurance there is against loneliness.[15]

AGM speeches and articles in *Home and Country* contain more and more rhetoric and less and less substance. They become very much about being part of this large and powerful movement, a communality of women, tolerant and friendly. In some way this also links up with moves in the 1950s to set up institutes on both air force bases and within mental hospitals. However, the need for tolerance was to be revoked at the sight of injustice as Lady Brunner NFWI Chairman argued at the 1956 AGM:

> So long as there is cruelty or harm to children and young people, as long as animals are ill treated; as long as there are ill designed shoddy goods on the market; as long as there is an avoidable hazard for young and old whether on the roads, or by accidents in the home or by food poisoning; as long as country people are badly in need of amenities they should share with townspeople and as long as we are bound by fellowship truth and justice we can afford to be intolerant about a lot of things.[16]

There is in this, I think, a line which is familiar in women's political activities (from women's involvement in nineteenth-century radical politics onwards), which is that women while accepting a primarily domestic sphere are, due to external circumstance, forced to become political, strident even, in order to carry out their socially defined domestic tasks. Thus women's domestic base was used to justify their demands for social reforms. In so doing rather than challenging women's association with domesticity, the meaning of domesticity was challenged, its boundaries were redefined. Domesticity became not passive but active and assertive. The political leanings of such an assertive domesticity, with its grounding in a notion of public housekeeping are by no means guaranteed however and were utilised by the Conservative Party. Bea Campbell, for example, records how the party's paper for women included in 1950 a husband praising his wife's housekeeping and wishing 'the Government were as good at national housekeeping as you are darling'.[17]

Whatever the major parties' attempts to appeal to women, the power of the ballot box, even with a relatively radical government, offered women little in the immediate post-war period. The Women's Institute Movement laid more and more emphasis on the social side of the Movement and in the never-had-it-so-good years, women turned to a sphere that did offered a space to carve out female expertise and control – consumerism.

Mica Nava has argued that:

Consumption has offered women new areas of authority and expertise; new sources of income, a new sense of consumer rights and one of the consequences of these developments has been a heightened awareness of entitlement outside the sphere of consumption which may well have contributed to the conditions for the emergence of modern feminism.[18]

This perception of consumption, offering women an area of authority, places a feminist interpretation on NFWI campaigns for consumer protection and acceptable standards of workmanship epitomised in a 1948 AGM resolution stating:

That this meeting deplores the poor quality of household goods and clothing produced for the home market and asks that available material be used to better advantage both as regards workmanship and design, so long as no action is taken that would in any way detract from the export market.[19]

What this indicates is a version of housewives not as passive consummers of any item in the market, but as discerning and critical buyers expressing their expertise. The consumerism of the NFWI in the 1950s, which *Home and Country* tried to instruct and guide its readers through, was for: domestic commodities, fridges and electric irons, which improve the circumstances of members everyday lives possibly reducing the burden of their domestic labour. The desire to acquire such commodities implies a rejection of the conditions of labour within the domestic sphere at a historically specific point in time. Feminism in the 1970s relied upon some women's belief that something different was possible, and attainable political action was perceived as a way of making these changes. However, to many women in the 1950s and certainly those in the WI, it was consumerism which offered the possibility of change. Compared to an acceptance of life and women's position as inevitable and unchanging such consumerism was at one level deeply and constantly subversive. It was also innately pragmatic. To quote Erica Carter, 'Consumerism not only offers but continually fulfils its promise of everyday solutions, albeit limited and partial ones, to problems whose origins lie elsewhere'.[20] It does offer at least some solutions and thus perhaps also legitimates the problems. Women in a patriarchal and capitalist society carve out their own spaces, their own alternative culture, but in that space allowed them by the dominant culture. Consumerism was such a space. It had been struggled for and deserves therefore to be celebrated rather than judged from a different historical specificity. Thus the feminism of the NFWI in the 1950s may lie in part in reworking a domestic version of femininity using consumerism, but it also involved issues and themes which were consistent with the earlier struggles over women's right to female-defined leisure and cultural space and over improving the conditions and elevating the status of rural women, particularly in their skilled work as unpaid domestic labourers. I shall therefore now explore in more detail the nature of the domesticity that the Women's Institute Movement espoused in the 1950s.

At the local level, WI activities at this time centred around the monthly meeting. Indeed in the 1950s, as Liz Stanley has pointed out,[21] they were one of the few all women's organisations to hold such meetings which were partly social, partly educational and partly about pressure group politics. As I explained above, individual institutes and county federations organised choirs, drama groups, specialist craft training, local markets for selling produce and many other events. The movement's perception of the socially acceptable domestic woman, which was advocated in such activities, was contradictory and in many respects quite radical. It operated within the notion of an 'equal but different' concept of marriage as had many late nineteenth and early twentieth-century feminists such as Josephine Butler and Mrs Fawcett. It incorporated a re-evaluation of domestic skills as different from, but just as significant as, male work. It was an ideal which women fought for in the 1920s and 1930s from a feminist perspective within the WI Movement and within the Labour Party,[22] and it was enshrined in the Beveridge Report. To many women at the time, it was a real step forward. I acknowledge that the 'equal but different' model ignores economic power relations and that it can be hi-jacked by the right to be both repressive for women and an argument for a reduction in welfare services on the assumption that women's caring role can expand infinitely, however women with a strong female culture, such as the WI provided, may use the 'equal but different' style of relationship for: contestation over equality of status, skill, and the significance of unwaged domestic labour as well as to challenge definitions of work within the capitalist production process. These contestations were more overtly explored by feminists in the campaign for Wages for House-work at a latter date. From NFWI's 'equal but different' perception of marriage and their insistence on the skilled status of domestic labour, the feminism of the following AGM resolution in 1957 can be understood:

Whilst grateful for the Budget concessions, this meeting realises that many men's working tools carry no purchase tax, and urges the Chancellor of the Exchequer as soon as possible to abolish the purchase tax on housewives kitchen utensils including electrical appliances.[23]

Women were to the NFWI skilled workers with a status equivalent to that of men. These ideas of skill were potentially expandable into other areas such as mothering.

Certainly the many faceted nature of the NFWI version of domestic womanhood is demonstrated by Barbara Kaye's novel, *Lychford to London Return*, first published in parts in *Home and Country* and then as a book in its own right[24]. The novel is structured around Lychford WI's outing to London to visit the NFWI handicrafts exhibition and a theatre. The book describes the activities of a variety of different women and the coach driver for whom the day's events are a significant turning or crisis point in their lives although not all of them attend the exhibition or play. Many of the issues of later 1970s feminism are tentatively raised in this book: domesticity, women's independence, sexuality and their complex relationship with consumerism are highlighted through individual women's lives. The book contains a fascinating contretemps about the problems that modern convenience housing can bring women as apparently when no longer tied to domesticity they use free time unwisely.[25] Principally the events of the novel are such to support a notion that a women's destiny is marriage. Two of the younger women start new relationships with men as a result of the day, one of which leads to marriage, whilst one of the older women spends the day readjusting her daughter to marriage and pregnancy (rather than a relationship with her hairdresser). She utters wonderful phrases like 'That's a wife's job, my girl, getting meals for her man',[26] or 'It doesn't seem to be you've anything to complain about with a husband getting on well like George is, and in a good, steady job. Didn't you tell me he was getting a rise'.[27] In the period of never-had-it-so-good what more could be wanted than an increase in pay? The book is also, however, an indication of the precariousness of the role of wife and mother and its questionable fulfilment for women. Although many of the resolutions are conservative, many of the questions raised are not. This, as Niamh Baker argues, is by no means unusual in fiction of the period and I would support her contention that possibly within such raising of questions lay the seeds of future feminism.[28] Furthermore in this post-war world, space is given to a view that life without men may, for women, have many advantages, for example:

> Miss Pennywell was a retired school-teacher. She lived in a neat, modern bungalow, one of half a dozen built by a local builder shortly before the war. Once before she had lost a friend through masculine intervention. For several years a fellow teacher had shared the bungalow with her and the two women had led an agreeable life, arguing about each other's work, eating snack meals, fussing about each other's health, and thanking heaven that they had never exchanged their freedom for a wedding ring and a lifetime of looking after some selfish, untidy, dominating man.[29]

It could not have been articulated better in the 1990s. Although this friendship had ended in the teacher marrying a middle-aged widower with three children, Miss Pennywell had remained in the village, as did her new WI friend who resisted the bullying of her brother to move, valuing female friendship and earning money from knitting, weaving and teas for tourists. Whether the WI reader in the 1950s privileged the questions asked or the resolution to this conflict is not easily ascertained.

Another interesting aspect of the book is the role played by Daisy, which seems to indicate a broadening notion of acceptable female sexuality. Daisy was a girl in her late twenties, with a 'reputation'; in the war she had been in the WAAF, done a great deal of hitchhiking and, to put it politely, played the field, even during a brief engagement. In the post-war period the reader discovers she has lived in London, both on her own and for six months with a 'second rate actor' called Charley before returning to work on the family farm. But she was unequivocally positively coded, friendly and pleasant, showing genuine concern for the driver of the coach whose wife was in a maternity hospital. Within the text she is not regarded as unacceptable by other women but with tolerant amusement. Her sexuality is seen as part of her salt-of-the-earth rural and 'natural' approach to life. Daisy, although notoriously late and untidy, has her feet on the ground and has learnt by her mistakes; having sown her wild oats she would like to settle down and have a family, something she is well on the way to achieving by the end of the novel. It might not seem at first glance a challenging version of sexuality but in the 1950s the notion that women even had wild oats to sow was a challenge to most definitions of femininity. Perhaps it was a post-Kinsey Report notion of the naturalness of female sexuality.[30] It is certainly a change from the 'beware of becoming tarnished goods' advice that was more frequently handed out to young girls at the time. The representation of Daisy, in the book, certainly compares very favourably with Julia Mercer whose airs and graces, negative attitude to having more than one child and desire for a lifestyle well beyond what her husband can afford, lead her to shoplifting. Although, Erica Carter has argued that for women their bodies may be a source of leisure and pleasure as an object of consumption and spending,[31] this is not a position that the Women's Institute Movement's ideology seemed to have space for. Alternatively, Julia's role in the story could be interpreted by the members reading the text as signifying that for many women the rural way of life, selected by their husbands, excluded them from the female pleasure of clothes and consumption on themselves. Institute women were destined for a more practical lot in life but many may have wished for more. The membership may have found ruralism at times restricting, but the nature of ruralism itself, as defined by the organisation, was changing.

The NFWI in the earlier half of the twentieth century was linked with definitions of Englishness because of the rural being perceived as the heart of the country, metaphorically. But this was a changing concept in the 1950s. The perception of countrywomen as the-salt-of-the-earth, in whatever country, lay at the heart of the NFWI's internationalism and also in their conflicting views of femininity. There were still elements of the nostalgic in their ruralism. *Home and Country* ran a competition entitled 'stories my grandmother told me'[32] and significantly there were the first WI local histories and scrapbooks in the 1950s, which one member described thus: 'In the WI Movement we are finding a good way to express our affection for our locality and our interest in the world around us through our local histories and scrapbooks'.[33] But this Englishness was contradictory and open to contestation; there was a sense of change. It was forward looking particularly in the response to the Coronation. The NFWI rejected the nostalgic elements of becoming 'New Elizabethans' in 1953, the Coronation year, in favour of creating a new heritage. Lady Brunner argues at the AGM:

> Today we begin entering a new reign which has to be given its own quality ... those of you with growing families must already have recognised this ... They look to a new era with its own excellence and virtue, its own poets and writers and musicians and painters, and they

will see that contemporary history is a rich and vivid heritage and an inspiration to posterity not a second hand rehash of individual splendours of the reigns of Queen Elizabeth 1 and Queen Victoria.[34]

The NFWI therefore, for their singing festival in 1953 and their drama festival in 1957 commissioned contemporary writers, rather than using a selection of the English classics. This heritage was about the arts and middle-class pursuits, indicative of the changing class emphasis of both the NFWI and rural areas. It was also in line with a wider perception of the nation or 'the people' as middle class epitomised by the myth of Macmillan reputedly saying, 'The class war is over and we have won'. The middle classes had been beneficiaries of the post-war welfare state in terms of: education, the arts and health and the post-war era also saw the improvement of amenities and services to rural England, especially in the Home Counties, much wider spread water and sewage services, electricity, telephones, for example, and the middle classes moved to villages they would not have considered acceptable in the pre-war era. This was probably responsible for a large increase in WI membership in the South in the 1950s accompanied by a shift towards a more middle-class perception of WI members.[35] The Women's Institute Movement for these new members was a way into rural life and a tradition of English womanhood which they were seen as wanting to adopt.

In 1955 *Home and Country* ran a brief series entitled 'Jottings of a New Member' which encapsulates this version of the membership. The 'jolly jotting' new member had absolutely no knowledge of country life. It is implied in the text that she was educated at a girls' private school. Her husband is an estate agent and they have four children well spaced out in the middle-class fashion of the time. They have moved to the countryside and live in a house created out of two workmen's cottages. This very middle class viewpoint would have been taboo in the pre-war WI when more emphasis would have been given to the workman's needs.[36] The family take up country living; keep hens known as 'the girls', the older children attend the local grammar schools and the mother joins the local WI, taken to her first meeting by an old schoolfriend whose husband works in the same estate agent's office as the jotting new member's. The style of the writing is a mixture of irony and humour which has a long tradition in women's writing and illuminates the gap between idealised image and reality in women's lives even around motherhood, for example: 'Decided to embroider little bunch of cherries on Polly's dress. I think it's enchanting but P. not thrilled. She'd rather I'd done her favourite vegetable, carrots'.[37] Her motherhood was invariably tortuous and despite the best of intentions her children remain a slightly mystifying, alien species.

The reader was invited to identify with the mystification and distance from the countryside that the new member experienced. Funny and interesting things were always happening and recounted in the jottings; after difficulty climbing a gate the following exchange takes place between the jotting new member and a local resident:

> Meekly handed him basket and obediently hauled my too much weight over 'hinge end', clasping to me at same time some newly gathered sprays of ivy, a few thistle heads and a charming dead fern. My friend eyed them with disfavour. 'You'd get better kindling than that down at the spinney'.
>
> Explained it was not kindling but decoration. Was going to put it in lovely old copper kettle and stand it on old oak chest ... 'That so?' The hedger grinned. 'You be the new people from London I suppose"
>
> By which he meant I was clearly not country born. True enough. And I already suspect as I plough way through twilight and mud to chicken run with evening feed that country life is going to take some getting used to.[38]

The local WI could be perceived as breaking her into country ways, identifying and clarifying English ruralism for her, giving her a sense of belonging, of community. Her hens and garden proving her commitment to an old style pre-war WI ruralism, while her flower arranging of bits of twig (which locals perceive merely as inferior kindling) indicated the change of concerns within the movement (and indeed with women generally at the time). The organisation's perception of rural life is not, in the post-war period prioritising food production or agriculture, significant elements in the pre-war Women's Institutes. Chickens and vegetable growing has a place, but pig clubs or concern over women agricultural worker's wages was no longer prioritised. For women such as this jotting member and many more who did not actually live there, the role of the countryside was changing to become a site, not of production but of recreation and leisure instead.

And yet maybe this flower arranging can be seen as an indicator of women's assertion of the right to space for themselves, hitherto a rarity for the majority of working-class and lower middle-class women in the WI, but without which the feminism of the 1960s and 1970s could never have existed. Predominantly, flower arranging produces a very temporary product since flowers rarely last more than a few days. This is a shift from the craft work encouraged by the WI in the 1920s and 1930s. The utility in flower arranging is nil, unlike the other manual skills, such as jam-making and patchwork, which the organisation encouraged. It serves no purpose, it is purely decorative. Thus it may be interpreted at one level as an assertion by women of their right to spend time in a leisure pursuit with aesthetic rather than utilitarian values. It can be argued, of course, that flower arranging is rather centred in the domestic. It can be seen as an example of how domestic tasks have ideologically expanded to counteract the reduction in domestic labour that new technology should have brought about. There has, for example, been almost no reduction in the time spent in housework and washing over the last hundred years despite new machinery.[39] Technology did increase housewives' power, choice, ability to prioritise and create their own spaces. In the 1950 these spaces were taken up by a number of things; women's organisations were certainly very important, so were new hobbies, skills and recreations.

In the 1960s and 1970s this space was used, perhaps by some, in more overtly political ways, but the carving out of that space away from directly productive domestic labour had, significantly, been done by women in the 1950s. Furthermore, there are interesting ideological encoding about housewifery in a pastime like flower arranging. It is a signifier of the structuring and the createdness of a home. It takes the natural and by an individual's skill and manipulations, it produces an image which predominantly encodes its own artificiality. Thus flower arranging may be able to be seen as women celebrating and emphasising their own, very significant, part in the structuring of the domestic sphere. This may otherwise have been perceived as having a natural base – women bear and breastfeed children but the creation of the structure, physical and ideological, perceived as home, does not naturally occur. It is formed, created, by women. From the historical specificity of the 1990s, the significant role played by women in structuring homes may seem obvious and no cause for celebration. Many feminists may want to see women rejecting this role, but others, such as in the Wages for Housework campaign, want its significance foregrounded and recognised. The post-war homes with electricity, water, sewage, the beginnings of technological service machines (Hoovers or electric irons and fridges), and internal or well lagged pipes, were seen by many women as a cause for celebration. A home of one's own, relying heavily on the post-war building programmes, was seen as desirable and well worth struggling for. It was a sphere of influence and control, however limited, however conditional on male approval and say so. It still provided a level of autonomy not on offer to these women elsewhere. Women's role in the struggle to have achieved this may well have been a cause for celebration as was their right to space to do more than service the basic requirements of this home. Significant in women's ability to achieve this space in their lives was of course, the compression of child-bearing years that was occurring partially due to the wider use of contraception in the post-war era.[40]

The jotting new member is also full of concern and interest in social issues and implicitly or explicitly the NFWI's role in them. The readership would be aware of the movement's numerous concerns over previous years; members of the NFWI were able to bask in a wonderful rural life thanks to the past efforts of the organisation. Hence she was involved in the birth of a neighbour's baby which bears out the benefit, to women, of midwives being able to administer analgesics, something the movement had struggled for since the 1930s. This may have paralleled a wider perception of womanhood in the 1950s as enjoying benefits struggled for by previous generations, such as the vote, family allowances and maternity services. The jottings relate the involvement of the new member in a variety of experiences which reiterates the importance of NFWI campaigns and AGM resolutions. The local papers published lurid details of a murder – censorship was an issue for the NFWI, as were American horror comics. The local significance of the national Federation of Women's Institutes' AGM issues was emphasised when the jotting new member found trippers leaving litter in a local field. Similarly, when her daughter's school tunic fell apart (she had not insisted on the proper British Design kitemark when buying it), an emphasis on the development of expertise in consumption was stressed. Her son was involved in a motorcycle accident and only saved from severe injury by wearing a crash helmet – the removal of purchase tax on which was an AGM resolution in 1954.[41] Thus the member was encouraged to look beyond her institute to see the significance of national campaigns. In this period, when the British Empire was being dismantled, the membership were also encouraged to look outward in an international sense and this is the final area to look at.

The NFWI espoused, as the Cold War developed, a notion of internationalism and links with other countries, particularly through their membership of The Associated Country Women of the World (ACWW) which held a tri-annual conference and a variety of fundraising campaigns, pennies for friendship being the most well known. Membership was open to all NFWI members and was able to give them a wider sense of belonging and identification with other women beyond the national membership. In interviews, members have expressed excitement at identifying other ACWW members by their badge and the sense of mutuality felt.[42] This internationalism had it roots in the inter-war years when the NFWI supported the League of Nations Union and the Women's International League for Peace and Freedom. Indeed in 1946, at the conclusion of the war, the NFWI had re-affirmed its between the wars commitment to peace with the following resolution:

> The members of the NFWI, recognising the important part women can play in promoting world peace and agricultural prosperity, pledge themselves to study the United Nations Organisation, and to work by every means in their power for the promotion of friendship between nations by making contact with individuals and organisations in other countries, either direct or through international organisations such as the Associated Country Women of the World.[43]

In 1954 a resolution was passed which added a new clause to NFWI, county federation and local WI rules giving power to all three levels 'To promote international understanding among countrywomen'.[44] NFWI National Executive members and representatives visited other countries and welcomed foreign visitors to their AGMs and Denman College. The countries were as diffuse as the USSR and Ceylon and accounts of these visits in *Home and Country* and more mundane ones by members at monthly meetings, are a significant facet of the movement in the post-war period. Similarly, penpals in other countries and the adoption of refugee families in the post-war period became popular with members and Institutes respectively. Yvonne Bowron from an Oxfordshire institute explained in 1956:

We have adopted a family of three living in a Displaced Persons Camp in Austria. It consists of a father and a mother and a boy of fifteen. Both father and son suffer from tuberculosis and therefore no country will accept them as émigrés, by sending them parcels from time to time, remembering their birthdays and writing ... we trust we may bring to them a little unexpected happiness.[45]

This may sound a little patronising but not when seen with other activities, such as the Denman College course on the history of apartheid in South Africa. All these activities assisted in breaking down and rejecting a dominant political construction of foreigners as Other. One of the first visits was to post-war Germany by Helena Deneke in order to 're-educate German women into organising themselves for the common good'.[46] I wonder at the ideological underpinning of this; by whom and as what was the common good defined? Equally questionable perhaps was the setting up, with personnel from the English NFWI, of a Women's Institute Movement in Malaya concurrently with the British Army taking a fairly reactionary role in the Malaysian civil war.

The WI appears not only to have rejected dominant political constructions of 'foreigner as other' but more radically to reject definitions of black as Other, as a story entitled 'Black Beauty', published in *Home and Country*, demonstrated. The story is about a mother taking her small child to hospital to have an eye operation. It is full of all the pathos that such stories can contain. The mother walks up the long drive to the hospital. Her son clutches her hand, steadily tighter, as she prepares to leave him with the nursing staff. (It is set in the 1950s prior to a combined re-appraisal of Bowlby and the potential saving on nursing staff resulting in mothers being encouraged to stay with their children in hospital.) The nurse who is to look after her child approached:

Coming down the corridor towards them was a nurse. She was black. A young African girl. And she was wonderfully beautiful, radiantly alive. Her white uniform emphasised her colour vividly ... Oh dear thought Mrs Martin nervously. Supposing Andrew says something awkward. But Andrew gazed with awe. 'Oh, Mummy', he breathed ecstatically at last, 'Isn't she beautiful'.[47]

This story, which won first prize in a short story competition, concludes with both mother and son confident and reassured as the young boy has been handed into the nurse's safekeeping. Although from a 1990s perspective this discourse of race may be seen as questionable, the black nurse is coded positively. In the 1950s when overt racism was growing, resulting in the 1960s immigration restrictions, this story is both challenging and potentially radical. As with so much of the organisation, the NFWI position on Englishness and a consequent perception of the non-English or Other is not easily determined but contradictory and open to a progressive reading.

The Women's Institute Movement in the 1950s was an organisation of half a million women who met, supported each other and campaigned about issues which were to their lives significant. Certainly it was a less overtly political organisation and less recognisably feminist than it had been in the pre-war period, but its provision of a female culture allowed a re-appraisal of domesticity and the development of a particularly female view of politics and internationalism that may be recognisable in the modern-day Women's Institute Movement.

NOTES

1. *Home and Country*, January 1954, p17 – this has been the NFWI monthly magazine since 1919.
2. E.P. Thompson, *The Making of the English Working Class*, Penguin, Harmondsworth 1963, p12.
3. M.R. Higonnet, *et al* (eds.), *Behind the Lines*, Yale University Press, New Haven 1987.
4. *Home and Country*, 9 March 1946, p13.
5. The Produce Guild was set up by the NFWI in 1939 to help rural women increase food production and preservation.
6. *Home and Country*, March 1946, p13.
7. *Home and Country*, March 1945, p9.
8. *Keeping Ourselves Informed*, NFWI publication, London 1981.
9. *The Times*, 20 April 1951.
10. *Home and Country*, 9 May 1954, p235.
11. D. Dutton, *British Politics since 1945 – the Rise and Fall of Consensus*, Blackwell, Oxford 1991, p49.
12. Cecily McCall, 'Our Village', NFWI publication, London 1956, in NFWI Publications file at organisation's national archives.
13. *Home and Country*, July 1957, p267.
14. *Home and Country*, February 1957, p52.
15. *Home and Country*, July 1957, p202.
16. *Home and Country*, July 1956, p225.

17. B. Campbell, *Iron Ladies*, Virago, London 1987.
18. M. Nava, 'Consumerism and its contradictions', in *Cultural Studies 2*, 1989.
19. *Keeping Ourselves Informed*, NFWI publication, London 1981, p24.
20. E. Carter, 'Alice in Consumer Wonderland', in M. Nava and A. McRobbie (eds.), *Gender and Generation*, Macmillan, London 1984, p213.
21. L. Stanley and A. Morley, *The Life and Death of Emily Wilding Davis*, Virago, London 1988, p145.
22 P. Thane, 'The Women of the British Labour Party and feminism 1906-1945', in H.L. Smith (ed.), *British Feminism in the Twentieth Century*, University of Massachusetts Press, Anheist, 1990.
23. *Keeping Ourselves Informed*, NFWI publication, London 1981, p26.
24. B. Kaye, *Lychford to London Return*, Macmillan, London 1955, p195.
25. *ibid.*, p27.
26. *ibid.*, p40.
27. *ibid.*, p41.
28. Niamh Baker, *Happily Ever After*, Macmillan, London 1989, p175.
29. *ibid.*, p30.
30. S. Jefferys, *Anticlimax*, Women's Press, London 1990, explores sexuality in the 1950s.
31. E. Carter, *op cit.*
32. *Home and Country*, March 1948, p12.
33. *Home and Country*, May 1952, p236.
34. *Home and Country*, July 1953, p221.
35. Organisation File in the NFWI archive.
36. *Home and Country*, January–July 1955.
37. *Home and Country*, January 1955, p16.
38. *Home and Country*, January 1955, p17.
39. Christine Hardyment, *From Mangle to Microwave – The Mechanisation of Housework*, Polity Press, Cambridge 1988.
40. E. Wilson, *Only Halfway to Paradise*, Tavistock, London 1980.
41. AGM file in NFWI archive.
42. Mrs Scott – oral interview of Sussex WI member in 1987 (name changed).
43. *Keeping Ourselves Informed*, NFWI publication, London 1981, p82-3.
44. *ibid.*
45. *Home and Country*, January 1956, p11.
46. *ibid.*
47. *Home and Country*, July 1958, p205.

AFTERWORD

The aim of this book has not been to chart every aspect of the Women's Institute Movement's history from its inception in 1915 until 1960. I am well aware that I have excluded many aspects of the Movement which others, particularly perhaps Women's Institute members themselves, would have considered important and included. My intention, however, as I explained in the introduction, has not been to provide an organisational history but to show how an all-women organisation like the NFWI can provide a space for feminism. My aim was thus to challenge both the construction of feminisms and the NFWI's past. I have therefore concentrated on some of the concerns of the Movement in the first forty-five years of their history. Many of these, such as agriculture and food production, became less significant over time, while others replaced them, such as the emphasis on the housewife's power and skill as a consumer in the 1950s. Other concerns such as craft work always had a place within the movement as did a pre-occupation with the rural home, although their emphasis and meaning varied over time as did the movement's perception of domesticity.

The social construction of femininity also changed in the first forty-five years of the Women's Institute Movement's history. The boundaries of acceptable femininity have changed. Overtly this is clear in terms of dress, work and sexuality, for example. The NFWI did not ever challenge women's domestic role in society head on, as second wave feminists did, but they did provide a space within which, in a variety of different ways, women of different class, region, marital and work status could challenge those boundaries of acceptable femininity and contribute towards their deconstruction. The NFWI fought to improve the material conditions of rural women's lives in a number of ways, in particular, improved housing, water and sewage which were very real needs for rural women as were analgesics for childbirth, equal pay and the removal of purchase tax on kitchen equipment. Some of their campaigns were not successful, such as the demand for sick pay for housewives to be included in the National Insurance scheme. However, participation in the campaigns may have politicised women, and arguably, it may have helped them see the circumstances of their lives not as inevitable but as structured and they may have began to question in whose interests they were structured.

Today they still campaign on women's issues, asserting that 'since the WI was established in the UK in 1915 it has been influential in voicing the concerns of British women – no matter how simple, how complex or how controversial'.[1] The 1991 AGM called for greater research and government funding for the treatment of endometriosis. They have recently completed a survey on carers, the conditions under which they care for others, the help they do or don't get from social services and their financial problems. They publicised their results by the holding of a conference on the issue in 1993.

I have argued that the movement provided in the period up to 1960 a space where women could develop their own potential away from the scrutiny of men, whether in a village institute meeting, the intrigue of a county or national executive, the AGM or Denman College. What women learned could vary from, how to run a meeting or organise fundraising to acting and directing in a play, or undertaking elaborate craftwork. But it all helped them to challenge the internalisation of their oppression. Such activities had the potential to allow women to work out, adopt or adhere to different, more female, value systems than those usually offered to them by society. Certainly re-appraisals of the significance and value of housework, of skill and of the distinction between art and craft were all part of this.

Challenging the status of housework always incorporated the right to leisure, whether at the yearly outing, at Denman College or at the social events organised by the local WI. The leisure side of the organisation still exists. The NFWI arranges holidays for members both in the summer and at Christmas; destinations in 1992 included Italy, Russia and Vermont.[2] Some county federations organise taster days for members in a variety of sports and hobbies as wide ranging as to include parachute jumping, riding and photography. As one member explains 'As a mother of young children it is important to have some time that's just for me and I gain a lot from the experience of the other women'.[3] That space for herself had been fought for by previous WI members. Rural women have now, particularly with improved private transport in the South of England, a wider variety of resources offering them what in the pre-war period the local WI provided. There are parent-teacher associations at local schools, mother and toddler classes and women's studies classes run by the

WEA. There is a tendency to meet in less formal groups – the National Childbirth Trust Coffee Morning – or local hobbies clubs. But the Women's Institute Movement still has its place as the membership figure of nearly 300,000 indicates.

The Women's Institute Movement continues to provide an alternative female cultural space for rural women to develop their own skills and an all-women sphere at local meetings, some of which now run with a crèche for younger members. Their present publicity leaflet claims 'The WI offers the opportunity for women to meet in a friendly atmosphere where they can develop new interests and acquire skills of value to themselves, their families and their communities'.[4] Paula Yates recently described joining her local WI, for *Good Housekeeping* in highly favourable terms. In an attempt to challenge the 'Jam and Jerusalem', image and with a background of a heated exchange over competition chutney, one member assured her 'It shows newcomers that we're not just a load of old biddies going on about jam – we jolly well care about pickles too'.[5]

However, some aspects of the movement are not perhaps as they were once perceived. Denman College, if not the spearhead of women's education that Cecily McCall had hoped, runs a wide range of courses from crafts to computing. However for those who attend, it still offers radical potential. Betty Burton, feminist author of over seven books including *Women are Bloody Marvellous*,[6] was a member of West Meon WI in Hampshire. It was at a Denman College course on 'The Place of the Thriller in Literature' that she gained the confidence to start writing. She realised 'not all authors are of the Somerset Maugham variety' and that it was possible for someone with her lack of formal education to write for a living'.[7] Thus the NFWI goes on providing space for women to carve out their own road to feminism.

As I said in my Introduction, the images of the Women's Institute Movement and recent feminism are not immediately congruous. However the present feminist movement has many divisions as, I have argued, it always had. Sheila Rowbotham points out:

> But two decades on it is incontrovertible that there are many feminist visions of the future we seek. There remains divisions of right and left, and there are differences between women based on class and race, for example. Other variations of circumstance – whether women are caring for children or other dependants, the nature of women's work, age or disability – can all effect how women define their needs.[8]

The NFWI thoughout its history has been defining the needs of rural women and helping women to meet those needs. At times these needs have overlapped with those verbalised by the more radical or overt strata of the feminist movement, over equal pay for example. Alternatively the Women's Institute Movement has at times, particularly over the issue of women's domestic role, been perceived to be in direct opposition to some forms of feminism. In recent years the splits within feminism over class, race, pornography and sexuality (to name only a few issues) have become more pronounced, no division more so, perhaps, as that between the middle-class – often academic – feminist and the mass of ordinary women. As someone who has worked within feminism and women's studies in higher education, whilst also trying to remain part of the networks of ordinary women which make the bringing up of small children bearable, I have felt this acutely. As ideas of post-feminism are mooted, as feminists as varied as Betty Friedan[9] and Ros Coward[10] begin to question the righteousness of a feminism which saw careers as representing freedom for women, maybe the time is ripe for a convergence of the feminisms of the Women's Institute and the products of post-1960s feminism. In order for this to happen a different narrative of the past is required, just as the NFWI required different narratives of its past at differing points in history. This then has been the objective of this book to help create a new version of feminism's past, a broader, more encompassing feminist tradition which will help extend its appeal now. For me, the Women's Institute Movement – creating an alternative female cultural space for rural women, campaigning to improve their material well-being and constantly challenging the socially constructed boundaries of femininity – offers an empowering tradition, a very suitable past for women today.

NOTES

1. Why the WI?, NFWI pamphlet, 1992.
2. *Home and Country*, August 1992, p17.
3. Why the WI?, NFWI pamphlet, 1992.
4. *ibid*.
5. *Good Housekeeping*, September 1992, p119.
6. Betty Burton, *Women are Bloody Marvelous*, London 1986.
7. *Home and Country*, July 1992, p15.
8. Sheila Rowbotham, *The Past is Before Us*, Penguin, Harmondsworth, 1989, p298.

9. Betty Friedan, *The Second Stage*, Michael Joseph, London 1982.
10. Ros Coward, *Our Treacherous Hearts*, Faber and Faber, London 1992.

APPENDIX 1

Six months of the Saynes Hill Programme for 1919 in which it was a
Sussex Federation prize winner for the best Programme

January 8th

'Good Better, Best
Never let it rest
Until the good better
and the better best.'

ANNUAL MEETING
Secretary's Report, Treasurer's Balance Sheet.
Adoption of Report and Balance Sheet.
Election of Committee by Ballot.
Talk: 'The House I should Like to live in,' Miss Churton
(Rural Housing Association)   Co-operative Tea

✻   ✻   ✻

Dressmaking and Stitchery classes will begin on January 27 at 2:30.
Miss Hadow Vice Chairman of the National Federation, will speak on
America at an open meeting on Wednesday, February 5th, at 6:30 p.m.
in the school.

✻   ✻   ✻

February 12th

'There are different ways of doing things,
As everyone supposes;
Some girls turn up their sleeves and work
While some turn up their noses.'

Discussion on Gardens and Small stock by Institute members.

Pigs, Miss Huddart; Gardens, Mrs Button; Rabbits, Miss Hill.
President's Report.
Demonstration Rabbit Skin Curing, Miss Hill.
Roll Call: 'What is most Wanted in the Village'.
Members' Stall   Co-operative Tea

* * *

March 12th

'Not till the hours of light return,
All we have built do we discern.'
– Mathew Arnold

Talk; 'Sussex Folk Lore and Tradition', Mrs Huddart.
President's report.
Competition: Best Made Blouse.
Entertainment.   Co-operative Tea. April 9th

'Character is property: it is the noblest of possessions.'
– Smiles.

Demonstration : Cheese Making, Miss Pilson.
Lecture: 'Citizenship', Miss Watkins.
President's Report.
Roll Call : 'What has the Women's Institute done for me?'
Exhibits: Old Shawls, Scarves and China.
Tea. Hostesses; The Committee.

* * *

May 14th

'Fair are the hills of Sussex, low and long,
and softly rounded as a mother's arm
about a cradle, dimpled naked, strong.'
– F.W. Bourdillon.

Garden Meeting.
Talk: 'Life in the Olden Days', Mrs Huddart.

President's Report.
May Day Customs, Miss Horn.
Guests: Wounded Soldiers.
Members' Stall.
Competition: May Garlands.
Tea Hostess:

*　　*　　*

June 4th

'Attempt the end, and
Never stand to doubt;
Nothing so hard but
Search will find it out.'
– Herrick

Garden Meeting at Cudwells.
Talk: 'House Crafts'.
President's Report.
Demonstration: Country Dances.
Exhibition: Toys and other things.
Guests: Wounded Soldiers.
Tea. Hostess: Mrs Huddart.
(Sussex Handbook of Women's Institutes, Brighton 1919)

APPENDIX 2

Breakdown of the 785 members of the Guild of Learners

Artificial Flower Makers	1	Milliners	34
Banner Makers	1	Needleworkers	56
Basket Makers	81	Leather Workers	137
Book Binders	5	Papier mâché Workers	5
Brush Bristlers	1	Pewter Workers	1
Carpenters	4	Potters	3
Chair Caners	68	Raffia Workers	100
Cobblers	8	Rug Workers	32
Crotchet Workers	12	Rush Workers	19
Designers	11	Slipper Makers	15
Dressmakers	41	Smockers	24
Dyers	16	Spinners	26
Embroiders	201	Stencillers	1
Etchers	1	String Shoe Makers	1
Fur craft Workers	57	Toy Makers	70
Glove Makers	187	Upholsterers	79
Household Jobbers	66	Weavers	31
Knitters	50	Woodcarvers	1
Lace Makers	19		

INDEX